GOD'S POWER TOOLS

FOR LIFE AND MINISTRY

BILL JUONI

A Practical Guide to the Gifts of the Holy Spirit

ISBN: 978-0-578-43946-4

First printing 2019

Printed in the United States of America

DEDICATION

This book is dedicated to my wife, Beth, and to my parents, Isaac and Aino Juoni.

Beth, you have been my loving wife and co-laborer in our years of serving the Lord together. First, serving the Lord together as laymen in the local church while I worked in retail management. Then, helping put me through Bible college by working full time while I worked part time and attended classes. Following that, serving the next twenty years as lead pastors. And now, since 1998, traveling together across the country and overseas in ministry as evangelists. What an exciting journey it's been serving the Lord together.

I also dedicate this book to my parents, who have now both passed away, my dad in 1992 and my mom in 1995. They brought me up in a loving Christian home and taught me the importance of serving Christ through their words and lives. I will forever be indebted to them for what they invested and instilled in me.

TABLE OF CONTENTS

ACKNOWLEDGMENTS

I would like to acknowledge and thank the many people who helped make this book possible.

First, I would like to thank my wife, Beth, who not only has been a faithful co-laborer in ministry, but also helped make this book possible through her computer knowledge, technical advice, and proofreading the manuscript.

Second, I would like to thank Kathy Curtis (www.christianbookformat.com) for editing and formatting the book and Brenda Haun (www.brendahdesigns.com) for designing the front and back covers. Without your expertise the book would not have been possible and you both were a pleasure and very easy to work with.

Third, I would like to thank all the pastors across the country who have invited us to come to their churches to conduct seminars on the gifts of the Holy Spirit. This book is the by-product of those seminars.

INTRODUCTION

For many decades and even centuries people built houses with hand tools. They used hand hammers, handsaws, and hand drills. They did it for years and even today you can still build a house with hand tools.

But oh, how much better to build with power tools! To have a nail gun, a power drill, and an electric saw. Yes, you can build with hand tools, but how much better it is to build with power tools.

I mentioned in my previous book, *More Power*, how Beth and I love to go camping when we go on vacation. One of the things we try to do while camping is to try to light the campfire with one match at the beginning of the week and to keep the fire going all week long, not using another match. To do this takes a lot of wood. For years I would cut the firewood with a "bucksaw," a type of hand saw. It took a lot of work. One day while back home I saw a man selling a power saw, a chainsaw, for only five dollars at a garage sale. Being a kind of "fix-it" guy, I figured I would buy it and fix it up. I bought it, fixed it, and we used it for years. It was like we entered a whole new world of cutting firewood. It was so much easier. After several years the chainsaw stopped working and could no longer be repaired. By then I was "hooked!" I went out and bought a brand-new chainsaw and we have used it ever since.

The gifts of the Holy Spirit are like God's power tools for life and ministry. Yes, a person can live a Christian life without the gifts of the Holy Spirit. But oh, how much better it is to have the gifts of the Holy Spirit. God's power tools for life and ministry.

This book is a practical handbook on the gifts of the Holy Spirit. It's like an operation manual for the gifts of the Holy Spirit to help us understand the gifts and how God can use us in the gifts.

When you get a power tool, you get an operation manual to help you understand the tool. To help you understand what it's for, what it's not for, what it can do, and how to use it.

This book is intended to be like an operation manual to help us understand what the gifts of the Holy Spirit are, what the gifts can do, and how to be used in the gifts, using Bible examples as well as everyday examples and illustrations from today.

While each gift is identified, explained, and illustrated, we realize that at times the operation of the gifts in life may blend together or overlap. In other words, to identify what gift it was that was manifested is not as important as the fact that a gift was manifested.

For example, if a sick person is healed, to split hairs over whether it was the gift of healing or a gift of miracles is not as important as the fact that a sick person was made well.

Also, one gift in operation may lead into another gift in operation. For example, a word of knowledge may lead into a word of wisdom, or a word of knowledge into a gift of healing, or a gift of discerning of spirits into a word of wisdom.

The main issue is that the gifts of the Holy Spirit are like God's power tools for life and ministry and are for today. Knowing about the gifts opens the door to being used in the gifts.

Chapter One

WELCOME TO THE GIFTS

Years ago I came across a story about Nordstrom's, the well-known department store chain. At the time of the story, Nordstrom's had stores in various parts of the country but none in the Chicago area. They decided to open a store in the Chicago area. No one thought much about it at the time because Sears and Roebuck was the giant retailer in the Chicago area and across the country.

The Nordstrom's store did very well, so they decided to open another store in the Chicago area. That store also did very well, so they opened another store in the area. The stores continued to do very well, and Nordstrom's continued to add new stores in the area. After a period of time, Nordstrom's caught up to and bypassed Sears and Roebuck as the number one retailer in the Chicago area. People were amazed.

A short time later a forum was held in the Chicago area with all the CEOs of the retailing giants in the area invited. The moderator of the forum went around the table asking the CEOs questions about their business practices. When the moderator got around to asking the CEO of Nordstrom's how they had caught up to and bypassed Sears and Roebuck as the number one retailer in the area, the CEO of Nordstrom's got up from his seat and walked out of the room. People wondered, *Where is he going? Did we offend him? Is he coming back?* Soon he returned to his seat carrying a booklet, sat down, laid the booklet on the table, and said, "This is our secret." People wondered, *What is this booklet?*

He then proceeded to tell them. He said, "We got ahold of the original operation manual for Sears and Roebuck and have followed it to the letter."

What had happened was Sears and Roebuck had begun to deviate from their original operation manual and they found themselves bypassed by someone who got ahold of their original operation manual and followed it to the letter.

We have been given the greatest operation manual that has ever been written, the Bible. It's the greatest operation manual for life, for ministry, and for the church.

In this book we want to look at what our operation manual tells us about the gifts of the Holy Spirit, God's power tools for life and ministry. It's meant to be like the operation manual you receive when you get a power tool.

In this book we will be looking at the gifts of the Holy Spirit listed in 1 Corinthians chapters 12 and 14.

"the word of wisdom through the Spirit, to another the word of knowledge through the same Spirit, to another faith by the same Spirit, to another gifts of healings by the same Spirit, to another the working

of miracles, to another prophecy, to another discerning of spirits, to another different kinds of tongues, to another the interpretation of tongues." (1 Corinthians 12:8-10, NKJV)

In this manual we will not be covering the ministry gifts found in Ephesians 4:7-13.

"And He Himself gave some to be apostles, some prophets, some evangelists, and some pastors and teachers." (Ephesians 4:11, NKJV)

Nor will we be covering the motivational gifts found in Romans 12:6-8.

"We have different gifts, according to the grace given us. If a man's gift is prophesying, let him use it in proportion to his faith. If it is serving, let him serve; if it is teaching, let him teach; if it is encouraging, let him encourage; if it is contributing to the needs of others, let him give generously; if it is leadership, let him govern diligently; if it is showing mercy, let him do it cheerfully." (Romans 12:6-8, NIV)

We will endeavor to cover the gifts of the Holy Spirit in a meaningful, understandable, and biblical way. Unfortunately, over the years many have been turned off to the gifts of the Holy Spirit because of some of the crazy, goofy, unbiblical things some have done under the guise of the "gifts of the Holy Spirit." Because of that, some have "thrown out the baby with the bathwater," wanting nothing to do with the gifts of the Holy Spirit.

Believers have done it, pastors have done it, and churches have done it. "The misuse of the gifts leads to lack of use and congregations can become Pentecostal in name only."[1] It's unfortunate, because the gifts of the Holy Spirit are biblical and can be a tremendous asset to life and ministry.

To reject the gifts of the Holy Spirit because of some "counterfeit" things some have done under the guise of the gifts of the Holy Spirit would be as senseless as rejecting the use of all $20 bills because some people have circulated "counterfeit" $20 bills.

Other pastors and churches have shied away from the gifts of the Holy Spirit, afraid that the gifts will scare visitors and new people away. The reality is that people are looking for the supernatural. Today people contact mediums, fortunetellers, psychics, horoscopes, etc., looking for the supernatural. "Our generation is not open to structured religion, but it will throw open the doors to the supernatural...the potential of the true Pentecostal church is boundless..."[2]

Ed Stetzer, on the faculty of Wheaton College (an evangelical college) and executive director of LifeWay Research, wrote in an article entitled, "Why Are Pentecostals Growing in Number?" dealing with the growth of Pentecostal churches:

"Pentecostals tend to be less "nominal" than other believers. The reason is often obvious — the baptism in the Holy Spirit... That helps make a more robust faith... stagnation is not as compatible with a real Spirit-filled experience... One of the dangers today is "bland evangelicalism"... Who wants to duplicate that? Nobody... Pentecostals attract people who are seeking something more than bland..."[3]

Yes, people want to feel safe and are scared when they don't understand something. When the gifts are explained and people understand what is happening, however, they are attracted to and ministered to by the gifts. I recall being at a general council a few years ago when one of the speakers, an evangelical, encouraged us as Pentecostals saying, "Don't stop being Pentecostal; just explain it."

We want to present the gifts of the Holy Spirit in not only a biblical way but also in an understandable way so whether someone is a new believer or has been a believer for a number of years, it is understandable. There is no probationary period for being used in the gifts of the Holy Spirit. "You do not have to be perfect, a minister, or have been saved for many years to exercise the gifts…"[4] The gifts are for new believers as well as for those who have been believers for years.

Also, the gifts are for any believer who needs help. "If you feel self-sufficient and spiritually superior, you may find it more difficult to see the gifts function."[5] On the other hand, if you realize how much you need Him and His help and desire His "power tools," they are available as He would choose to disperse them.

REVIEW AND DISCUSSION QUESTIONS

1. Why is the Bible referred to as our "operation manual?"

2. Why have some people rejected the gifts of the Holy Spirit?

3. Why are some people afraid of the gifts of the Holy Spirit?

4. Why do you believe the gifts of the Holy Spirit are for today?

5. How can a safe environment be provided regarding the gifts of the Holy Spirit?

Chapter Two

THE NEED TO KNOW
ABOUT THE GIFTS

∂ℓℓ

It's very biblical to know about and learn about the gifts of the Holy Spirit.

Jesus conducted His earthly ministry through the gifts of the Holy Spirit. In Philippians 2 Paul tells us that when Jesus left heaven to come to earth, He emptied Himself of His divine powers and attributes to become one of us.

"but emptied himself, by taking the form of a servant, being born in the likeness of men." (Philippians 2:7, ESV)

"The phrase 'emptied himself' in the Greek is *ekenosen* (from *kenosis*), which literally means he 'emptied himself,' or 'made himself nothing.' This does not mean that Jesus gave up His deity (i.e., his nature as fully God). It means He voluntarily laid aside the privilege of His limitless existence as God, including His heavenly glory, position, riches, rights, and the use of His attributes as God. This 'emptying of Himself' also meant taking on human suffering, misunderstanding, mistreatment, hatred, and in the end, the curse of death on the cross."[1]

He was sinless but one of us. So how did Jesus conduct His earthly ministry? It was through the power of the Holy Spirit. The same Holy Spirit that is available to us today. In Acts 10:38 we are told,

"how God anointed Jesus of Nazareth with the Holy Spirit and power, and how He went around doing good and healing all who were under the power of the devil, because God was with Him." (Acts 10:38, NIV)

In Matthew 3:16 we read,

"And when Jesus was baptized, immediately he went up from the water, and behold, the heavens were opened to Him, and He saw the Spirit of God descending like a dove and coming to rest on Him." (Matthew 3:16, ESV)

"Everything Jesus did — His preaching, His healings, His suffering, His victory over sin and Satan's power — He did by the power of the Holy Spirit. Even though He was fully God, He willingly laid aside and limited His rights and privileges as God. In becoming fully human, He had to operate the same way we must — as people dependent on God's Holy Spirit. If Jesus could do nothing apart from the power of the Holy Spirit, how much more do we need the Spirit's power? The Spirit equipped and worked powerfully through Jesus to accomplish God's plan... Jesus Himself would later baptize His followers with the Holy Spirit so that they too might have the Spirit's power to accomplish His purposes..."[2]

The Early Church conducted its ministry through the power and gifts of the Holy Spirit. The same Holy Spirit that is available to us today. The secret to the Early Church wasn't the size of their churches, the size of their buildings, or the culture they were in. Their secret was the power and working of the Holy Spirit.

Paul said in 1 Corinthians 12:1,

"Now concerning spiritual gifts, brethren, I do not want you to be ignorant." (1 Corinthians 12:1, NKJV)

The ESV translation says,

"Now concerning spiritual gifts, brothers, I do not want you to be uninformed." (1 Corinthians 12:1, ESV)

"He is not suggesting the Corinthians were stupid or below normal in mentality."[3] Paul simply wanted the believers in Corinth to know about the gifts of the Holy Spirit. Paul then went on to write about the gifts of the Holy Spirit in 1 Corinthians chapters 12 and 14.

In the middle of his writing on the gifts of the Holy Spirit, Paul writes 1 Corinthians 13, known as the "love chapter." In Paul's writing to the church in Corinth, he was writing a letter as we would write a letter today. There were no chapter divisions; these were added later. It was all one letter. So right in the middle of his writing on the gifts of the Holy Spirit, Paul writes about love.

The purpose being, the gifts were to be ministered in love by people who love. He goes on to write that without love they are: hallow, empty, noise, and nothing.

"If I speak in the tongues of men and of angels, but have not love, I am only a resounding gong or a clanging cymbal. If I have the gift of prophecy and can fathom all mysteries and all knowledge, and if I have faith that can move mountains, but have not love, I am nothing. If I give all I possess to the poor and surrender my body to the flames, but have not love, I gain nothing." (1 Corinthians 13:1-3, NIV)

"The absence of love nullifies the effectiveness of even the most powerful of the gifts."[4]

PRINCIPLES REGARDING THE GIFTS OF THE HOLY SPIRIT

They Are Gifts

"There are different kinds of gifts, but the same Spirit." (1 Corinthians 12:4, NIV)

We need to always remember, they are gifts. "They have nothing to do with human ability, natural talent, or learned behavior…"[5] The gifts of the Holy Spirit are not carefully planned actions or well thought-out words. They are gifts.

We also need to remember, we do not earn them or deserve them. They are gifts. In fact being used in a gift of the Holy Spirit is not a sign of spirituality or spiritual maturity. It's a sign that someone was open and willing to step out in faith and God was able to use them.

"The gifts are not 'extras' or 'bonuses' for those who are super-spiritual… The gifts do not make one believer superior to others or more favored of God. The gifts simply indicate the believer is aware of the tools God has supplied and is willing to use them as God directs."[6]

"They are not rewards or achievements or even trophies of spirituality. Rather, they are undeserved and imparted by the will of God for the good of the whole church."[7] "God has a real problem. He has no perfect Christians to use."[8]

This explains why at times people have been used in gifts of the Holy Spirit who still may have issues in their life they have not yet overcome. Some have asked, "How can God use them? They still _____ (*and they name an issue in that person's life*)." "They (*the gifts*) do not belong to the individual; neither do they make the individual whom God uses to minister the gifts infallible or holy."[9]

Saul prophesied in 1 Samuel 19:18-24. During this time Saul was pursuing David, which was not right. The ESV Fire Bible notes on 1 Samuel 19:21 say, "This passage makes it clear that being empowered by the Holy Spirit for prophecy or any other spiritual activity does not always mean that the person has a right relationship with God. At this time Saul was in rebellion against God."[10]

Jesus said,

"On that day many will say to me, 'Lord, Lord, did we not prophesy in your name, and cast out demons in your name, and do mighty works in your name?' And then I will declare to them, 'I never knew you; depart from me, you workers of lawlessness.' " (Matthew 7:22-23, ESV)

The ESV Fire Bible notes on Spiritual Gifts for Believers says, "It is unbiblical and unwise to assume that because someone exercises a gift in an outwardly impressive way such as healing or prophecy, that person is more spiritual than those with less spectacular gifts. In fact, "possessing" a gift does not mean that God approves of all that person does or teaches. Spiritual gifts must not be confused with the fruit of the Spirit (found in Galatians 5:22-23), which relate more directly to Christian character and spiritual growth."[11]

Obviously the ideal is for a person to have a good testimony of a victorious Christian life so these questions are minimized.

We also need to remember that we don't own the gifts of the Holy Spirit. God uses us in the gifts but we don't own them. We don't possess them. These are gifts given at a specific moment or time for a specific situation. "They are not resident in individuals, but are manifested through them as the Holy Spirit requires and inspires."[12] Regarding the gifts of the Holy Spirit in 1 Corinthians 12 and 14, we don't own a gift or have a gift; we are used in the gifts.

When referring to the motivational gifts found in Romans 12:6-8 and the ministry gifts found in Ephesians 4:11, we could say a person owns these gifts. For example, regarding the ministry gifts; a person is called to be a pastor, a prophet, etc. Or regarding the motivational gifts; a person has the gift of mercy, or the gift of leadership, etc. This is how they are by nature, how they are "wired." They have these gifts. But regarding the gifts of the Holy Spirit found in 1 Corinthians 12 and 14, we don't own these gifts; we are used in these gifts.

Also, being used in a gift isn't the same as being called to a certain ministry. For example, being used by the Spirit to give a prophetic word doesn't make someone a prophet. There is a specific calling to be a prophet, which is different than someone being used to give a prophetic message at a particular time or for a particular situation. It also doesn't mean they have the motivational gift of prophecy, where a person leans more toward seeing things as "black and white" and being direct in personality and nature.

So if we don't own any of the gifts of the Holy Spirit listed in 1 Corinthians 12 and 14, this then raises the question as to why certain people are often used in the same gift. The answer is they have learned to be open to that gift and to step out in faith to be used in that gift. The more a person is used in a certain gift, the easier it is for them to recognize that God wants to use them and to step out in faith and be used in that gift. "Once a person has been used of the Spirit to manifest a particular gift, it is much easier for that believer to minister in a similar manner again and again."[13]

No matter how often a person is used in a certain gift, however, they don't own that gift. They cannot just pull it out and be used whenever they desire. A person can only be used whenever God wants to use them at a specific time for a specific situation.

We are like reflectors. Reflectors don't possess the light. They don't have the light in themselves. They only reflect the light.

We don't possess the gifts. We don't have them in ourselves. We reflect the gifts from God. We are used in the gifts by God.

The Gifts Come from the Same God

"There are different kinds of gifts, but the same Spirit. There are different kinds of service, but the same Lord...the same God works all of them." (1 Corinthians 12:4-6, NIV)

All the gifts come from the same God.

The Gifts Are Given for Common Good

"The manifestation of the Spirit is given for the common good." (1 Corinthians 12:7, NIV)

The New King James Version says, "for the profit of all." The gifts of the Spirit are not given to destroy or tear down other individuals. They are given for "good," for "profit" of all. They also are not given for someone to take advantage of others. They are given for everyone's benefit. Notice the key words "common good," "profit of all."

The gifts of the Holy Spirit are to: (1) glorify God, (2) build the Church, and (3) reach the lost.

The Gifts Are Given As the Spirit Determines

"All these are the work of one and the same Spirit, and he gives them to each one, just as he determines." (1 Corinthians 12:11, NIV)

"Given" means "for a special situation or moment," not as a permanent possession. Notice also they are given as the Spirit determines, not as we determine. We do not pick and choose. It's as the Spirit determines.

Not All Are Used in the Same Gifts

God uses different people in different gifts. This is described in 1 Corinthians 12:12-30. Here Paul illustrates this by comparing the body of Christ, the Church, to a human body. Not all parts of the human body have the same function. The various parts have different functions and purposes, each contributing their part, which makes the body function as it should.

So it is with the gifts of the Holy Spirit. God uses different people in different gifts and together the body of Christ can function as it should.

Desire the Greater Gifts

"But eagerly desire the greater gifts." (1 Corinthians 12:31, NIV)

I remember a Bible school instructor asking the question, "What's the greatest gift?" The answer was, "The gift that is needed at the time."

For example, if we don't know what to do, the greatest gift is a word of wisdom. If there has just been a message in tongues, the greatest gift is an interpretation of a message in tongues.

The greatest gift is the gift that is needed at the time.

Desire Spiritual Gifts

"Eagerly desire spiritual gifts." (1 Corinthians 14:1, NIV)

In the Greek the word for "desire" is a strong word. "The Greek says that we should 'crave' or 'earnestly contend' for the spiritual gifts."[14] It has the same meaning as the word used to desire God. Paul encourages us to eagerly desire to be used in the gifts of the Holy Spirit.

This desire should not only be that God would use us in the gifts in the church and in a worship service, which was the context of what Paul was addressing in 1 Corinthians 12 and 14, but also that God would release the gifts of the Holy Spirit in our everyday lives Monday through Saturday as well.

THE GIFTS ARE TO OPERATE IN ORDER

"For God is not a God of disorder but of peace." (1 Corinthians 14:33, NIV)

"But everything should be done in a fitting and orderly way." (1 Corinthians 14:40, NIV)

The gifts of the Holy Spirit are to operate in an orderly way. They were not to be a source of chaos, confusion, and disorder. More will be said about this later in the book.

THE GIFTS ARE SUBJECT TO THE CONTROL OF THE INDIVIDUAL

"The spirits of prophets are subject to the control of prophets." (1 Corinthians 14:32, NIV)

While this verse specifically deals with the gift of prophecy, the principle applies to all the gifts.

First of all, God will not force anyone to be used in a gift of the Holy Spirit. We must yield ourself to be used.

Secondly, a person is not "out of control" when they are going to be or are being used in a gift of the Holy Spirit. For example, a person can wait for an appropriate moment in the service to manifest a voice gift. More will be said about that later in the book.

THE GIFTS ARE NOT TO BE FORBIDDEN

"Do not forbid speaking in tongues." (1 Corinthians 14:39, NIV)

While this verse specifically deals with the gift of giving a message in tongues, the principle can be applied to all the gifts. The gifts were not to be forbidden. The gifts of the Holy Spirit were to be desired not forbidden. "Nowhere does he (*Paul*) try to eliminate or discourage the use of the gifts."[15]

Paul said,

"Desire spiritual gifts." (1 Corinthians 14:1, NIV)

Paul wanted the believers in Corinth to not only know about the gifts of the Holy Spirit but to also desire the gifts of the Holy Spirit. God wants us to know about the gifts of the Holy Spirit and to desire to be used in the gifts.

First we need to know about the gifts of the Holy Spirit. Knowing about the gifts will then lead to an awareness of the gifts. An awareness of the gifts will then lead to our being open to God using us in the gifts of the Holy Spirit. Being open to being used in the gifts will then lead to being used in the gifts.

We need to start by knowing about the gifts.

REVIEW AND DISCUSSION QUESTIONS

1. Why is it important to know about the gifts of the Holy Spirit?

2. What is the connection between love and the gifts of the Holy Spirit?

3. What does "the gifts are given" mean?

4. Why are some people often used in the same gift?

5. Why are the gifts not to be forbidden?

Chapter Three

THE NEED FOR THE BAPTISM IN THE HOLY SPIRIT

Could a person who is not baptized in the Holy Spirit possibly be used in gifts of the Holy Spirit? Is it possible? The biblical answer would have to be "yes."

As we look at the Old Testament we see most of the gifts manifested at times but only rarely and by only a few select individuals. For example, the Bible says Saul prophesied,

"And the Spirit of God came upon him also and as he went he prophesied." (1 Samuel 19:23, ESV)

God even used a donkey on one occasion to give a message.

"And the donkey said to Balaam, 'Am I not your donkey, on which you have ridden all your life long to this day? Is it my habit to treat you this way?' " (Numbers 22:30, ESV)

The gifts were manifested in the Old Testament and this was before Pentecost and the outpouring of the baptism in the Holy Spirit. The only two gifts not found in the Old Testament are "a message in tongues" and "an interpretation of a message in tongues." All the other seven gifts were manifested in the Old Testament at times but only by a very few select individuals.

In the Old Testament the Holy Spirit came upon individuals.

"But the Spirit of the Lord came upon Gideon." (Judges 6:34, NKJV)

In the New Testament after Jesus' resurrection, but before Pentecost, the Holy Spirit dwelt within believers.

"He breathed on them and said to them, 'Receive the Holy Spirit.' " (John 20:22, ESV)

After Pentecost the Holy Spirit filled and overflowed in believers who were baptized in the Holy Spirit.

"And they were all filled with the Holy Spirit and began to speak in other tongues as the Spirit gave them utterance." (Acts 2:4, ESV)

It can be illustrated in this way. If you put a glass under a faucet upside down and turn the water on, the water comes on the glass. Like the Holy Spirit came upon certain Old Testament individuals. If you put the glass right side up under the faucet and turn it on, the water dwells in the glass. Like the Holy Spirit dwells in all believers after Jesus' resurrection. If you continue to fill the glass so it overflows, this represents the baptism in the Holy Spirit.

After Pentecost and the baptism in the Holy Spirit, you find the gifts in operation often and by many. The baptism in the Holy Spirit is a gateway to the gifts of the Holy Spirit; increasing the frequency, the awareness, the openness, and opportunity to be used in the gifts.

The baptism in the Holy Spirit increases our spiritual sensitivity, making us more aware of the things of the Spirit. It's like rotating a television antenna to get better reception. When we are baptized in the Holy Spirit and regularly pray in the Spirit, we become more sensitive to the Holy Spirit.

Pastor Jeff Leake shared this story in his book, *Power for Life*. "In October 2012, Ron Johnson had traveled from his home in Orlando, Florida, to attend a pastor's roundtable in Huntsville, Alabama. After the first day of meetings was over, Ron began to feel a deep uneasiness in his spirit. Something wasn't right. He went to his room and began to pray in the Spirit, in tongues, seeking the reason he felt so uneasy. As he prayed, he felt a strong urge to leave Huntsville immediately. He called his wife and said, 'Please change my plane ticket. I want to leave right away.' He then explained to his colleagues that he needed to leave immediately. He checked out of the hotel, traveled to the airport, and stayed the night at a hotel near the airport so he could fly out to Orlando the next day. During the night, a tornado blew through Huntsville and it touched down just outside the hotel where the roundtable was being held. It struck the hotel that night and the point of impact was the very room where Ron had been staying. If Ron had remained, he most likely would have been killed. The other pastors were staying several floors below and successfully weathered the storm without injury by crawling under the staircase in the hallway. As Ron flew out the next morning, he was thanking God for the gift of the Holy Spirit. The baptism in the Holy Spirit and praying in the Spirit makes us more sensitive to the information the Holy Spirit wants to give us. It makes us more aware of His leadings and His promptings and this is a key to functioning in the gifts of the Holy Spirit."[1]

I heard this illustration at a conference. Suppose you had a group of believers from various backgrounds standing together visiting. Among them are some who are baptized in the Holy Spirit. Suddenly someone runs up to them and says there is a demon-possessed man outside. Who are the most apt to go out there? It would be those who are baptized in the Holy Spirit. They would be the most apt to say, "Let's go take care of this."

If a person has a problem accepting the baptism in the Holy Spirit and speaking in tongues, they will most likely have a problem being open to the gifts of the Holy Spirit and other things of the Spirit. On the other hand, if they are baptized in the Holy Spirit, they are familiar with and open to the things of the Spirit. For them the gifts of the Holy Spirit are not a big step.

I remember being at a conference where the speaker said, "Let's start with something easy, the baptism in the Holy Spirit and speaking in other tongues, and then go on to other things. There is more after the baptism in the Holy Spirit." The baptism in the Holy Spirit is a gateway to the supernatural.

In my book on the baptism in the Holy Spirit, *More Power*, I shared Dr. George Wood's account of ministering in a large Assemblies of God church in a Middle Eastern country and the application he made. The account said,

> "When the building emptied of believers, the pastor explained that hundreds of Muslims were at that moment gathering outside, waiting for the doors to reopen. Why were they coming? Because they knew the Christians prayed for the sick and cast out demons. Dr. Wood said, 'In that church, the question of whether we need or do not need the baptism in the Holy Spirit does not even come up. When you are confronting powerful, evil forces; invading hostile, enemy territory; confronting situations individuals have no human answers for; and where positive thinking and self-help techniques do not work—you must have a power that comes from God.' The baptism in the Holy Spirit is the gateway to the supernatural."[2]

It's not just in the Middle East, but today we too are confronting powerful evil forces, we too are invading hostile enemy territory, we too are confronting situations individuals have no human answers for, and we too are facing situations where positive thinking and self-help techniques do not work. We too must have a power that comes from God. Jesus words to His disciples still apply to us today!

Jesus said,

> *"Heal the sick, cleanse the lepers, raise the dead, cast out demons. Freely you have received, freely give."* (Matthew 10:8, NKJV)

"Go into all the world and preach the gospel to every creature. He who believes and is baptized will be saved but he who does not believe will be condemned. And these signs will follow those who believe. In my name they will cast out demons; they will speak with new tongues; they will take up serpents; and if they drink anything deadly, it will by no means hurt them; they will lay hands on the sick, and they will recover." (Mark 16:15-18, NKJV)

Let's start with the baptism in the Holy Spirit, the gateway to the supernatural. "The Holy Spirit has all the power we need, all the timely information we need, and all of the solutions we need for any and all situations we face."[3] The Holy Spirit is smarter than we are and knows more than we know.

In the following chapters we're going to look at the supernatural gifts of the Holy Spirit, breaking them into three groups of three each:

- the mind of God gifts
- the power of God gifts
- the voice of God gifts

Regarding each gift, we will look at:

- what the gift is
- what the gift is not
- Bible examples of the gift in operation
- examples of the gift in operation today
- how to be used in that gift

REVIEW AND DISCUSSION QUESTIONS

1. Give some examples of gifts of the Holy Spirit found in the Old Testament.

2. What two gifts of the Holy Spirit are not found in the Old Testament?

3. Why is the baptism in the Holy Spirit important in being used in the gifts of the Holy Spirit?

4. How does the baptism in the Holy Spirit open the door to being used in the gifts of the Holy Spirit?

5. Is the baptism in the Holy Spirit just a goal or is it a gateway? Explain.

Chapter Four

WORD OF WISDOM

"For to one is given the word of wisdom through the Spirit." (1 Corinthians 12:8, NKJV)

WHAT IS THE GIFT OF A WORD OF WISDOM?

A word of wisdom is a supernatural revelation from God to man giving a solution to a problem we did not have an answer for. A word of wisdom answers the questions, "What do I do?" "How do I handle this?" This gift deals with action. It's God supernaturally revealing practical instruction to a person regarding what to do in a specific situation. "A word of wisdom will highlight the best possible course of action to take."[1]

Being given a word of wisdom for a specific situation does not make a person permanently wise. It's a word of wisdom for a specific situation and moment.

WHAT THE GIFT OF A WORD OF WISDOM IS NOT

A word of wisdom is not guessing what to do. It's not one's opinion on what to do. It has nothing to do with one's natural wisdom in knowing what to do or their overall wisdom. It has nothing to do with one's IQ. It is not an accumulation of wisdom. "He (*God*) gives just enough for the present situation."[2]

BIBLE EXAMPLES OF THE GIFT OF A WORD OF WISDOM

Jesus' Answer Regarding Paying Taxes

In Luke 20:20-26 we read where Jesus is being questioned by the Pharisees regarding paying taxes. They were trying to catch Him saying something against the government so they could deliver Him to the authorities. They asked, "Is it lawful for us to pay taxes to Caesar or not?" Jesus says, "Show me a denarius. Whose image and inscription does it have?" They answered, "Caesar's." Jesus said to them, "Render therefore to Caesar the things that are Caesar's, and to God the things that are God's."

The Holy Spirit gave Jesus a word of wisdom as to how to answer the Pharisees' question.

The Early Church Regarding Food Distribution

In Acts 16:1-4 we read how the Early Church was rapidly growing and the Grecian widows began complaining that they were being left out of the food distribution. The apostles said they couldn't leave praying and ministering the Word to do the food distribution.

The Holy Spirit then gave the Early Church a word of wisdom as to what to do. They said let's appoint seven men full of the Holy Spirit to handle the food distribution so we can continue ministering the Word and praying. This led to the selection of the first deacons.

God gave the Early Church leaders a word of wisdom as to what to do.

The Early Church Regarding What to Do About the Gentiles

In Acts 15:13-21 we read how the Early Church was growing and many Gentiles were coming to Christ. The question arose as to what was to be required of the Gentiles. Were they to be expected to be circumcised and to keep the Jewish laws and traditions?

As the Early Church was discussing this issue, James spoke up and said,

> *"We should not make it difficult for the Gentiles who are turning to God. Instead we should write to them, telling them to abstain from food polluted by idols, from sexual immorality, from the meat of strangled animals and from blood."* (Acts 15:19-20, NIV)

God gave James a word of wisdom and the problem was solved.

Paul Before the Council

In Acts 23 we read where Paul has been brought before the council, falsely accused by the jealous, angry Jews of desecrating the temple. As Paul stood before the council, the Bible says,

41

"Now when Paul perceived that one part were Sadducees and the other Pharisees, he cried out in the council, 'Brothers, I am a Pharisee, a son of Pharisees. It is with respect to the hope and the resurrection of the dead that I am on trial.' " (Acts 23:6, ESV)

This caused a dissention among the council because some were Pharisees and others were Sadducees. The dissention became so great that the Roman tribune had to end the trial before the council.

God gave Paul a word of wisdom.

EXAMPLES TODAY OF THE GIFT OF A WORD OF WISDOM

In Church Leadership

Some examples today would perhaps be in a church board meeting as the board is discussing what to do regarding an issue. God can give one of the board members a word of wisdom as to what to do. Perhaps the board is discussing how to reach their area for Christ and God gives someone a word of wisdom as to what to do. Also, it could happen in a church business meeting.

Our Transition into This Ministry

I remember when we were getting ready to transition from pastoral ministry to traveling as evangelists. I needed to call our national office to ask them to take me off the pastor directory and to put me into the evangelist listing. I called the national office and asked them to make the change. I will never forget the secretary's response. She made the change and then said, "Now you're one of them." I said, "Is that it?" She said, "Yes, you're one of them." I asked, "Don't I get a book or a manual?" She said, "No, you're one of them." There was no book, no manual. But God has given a word of wisdom when it has been needed to do what He has called us to do.

Solving Our Product Table Issue

Another example was when people were asking at our product table if we accepted credit cards. At that time we only accepted cash and checks. We decided, with all the people who were asking, we needed to get set up to accept credit cards. We went to our local bank and asked if they could get us set up to accept credit cards. They assured us they could and we filled out the necessary paperwork and turned it in. We waited for weeks and would periodically check on the progress at the bank. The bank couldn't understand what the delay was. One day as I was praying about the situation, I believe the Lord gave me a word of wisdom. The Lord said, "Check at your local credit union." That day I went to the local credit union and told them what we wanted to do. They said they could set us up and within a few days we were set up to receive credit cards. God gave a word of wisdom.

Warning Regarding a Car Repair

Not only can God give a word of wisdom regarding ministry issues, but also regarding practical life issues. I remember working on our car on a cold winter day when we were pastoring in Minnesota. I needed to replace the condenser in the distributor. I bought the new part and began to replace the defective one. I removed the old part and when I went to install the new part, my fingers were cold, and I dropped one of the small screws into a hole in the distributor. It fell out of sight, down into the distributor shaft. I figured, *What problem can a little screw cause? I'll just use one of the old screws to install the new condenser.* A voice was saying, *Get the screw out.* It was God attempting to give me a word of wisdom. I kept thinking, *What harm can a little screw do?* I put the new part in with the old screw, put everything back together, and started the car. Suddenly I heard a noise that was not a good noise to hear! The little screw that had fallen down into the distributor had fallen to where the gears are at the bottom of the distributor shaft and had gotten stuck in the gears and bent the distributor shaft. Now I needed to get a whole new distributor. God had tried to give me a word of wisdom but I ignored it.

HOW TO RECEIVE A WORD OF WISDOM

A word of wisdom can be received in a variety of ways. A common way a word of wisdom is received is by sensing this is the thing to do. You get an inner sense from the Holy Spirit of the direction to go in.

Another way a word of wisdom can be received is an idea comes into your mind. This doesn't mean that every idea that comes to mind is from God. We need to learn to discern, usually by trial and error, what it's like when God is giving us an idea versus an idea that is just passing through our mind.

Still another way God can give a word of wisdom is through a vision or a dream. The difference between a dream and a vision is a dream is what you get when you are sleeping. A vision is what you get when you are awake. Does this mean every dream is from God? No, some dreams are the result of what you have been thinking about the day before or the result of what you ate the night before. On the other hand, God can give you a word of wisdom through a dream or vision.

I remember hearing the testimony of R. G. LeTourneau, the Christian businessman and inventor who, among his many other inventions, invented the giant earth-moving machine used in road construction and mining. He said God showed him in a dream how to build the machine.

Many people have received a word of wisdom and didn't even realize it or acknowledge it. They just thought they had a great idea when in reality it was not their great idea, but God giving them a word of wisdom in their situation. There are times we may not even realize until later that God gave us a word of wisdom in a certain situation. A word of wisdom does not generally come like being struck with a bolt of lightning or giving us goose bumps. Often it's a thought or an idea that comes from God. There are times God has tried to give someone a word of wisdom and they have dismissed it as a fleeting thought without giving it consideration. There are other times when God has given us a word of wisdom and we have said, "I just had a great idea"; not realizing it was not us but it was God giving us a word of wisdom.

We need to be sensitive to what God may be trying to tell us in the midst of our situation. It may be a word of wisdom, God showing us what to do in a particular situation.

REVIEW AND DISCUSSION QUESTIONS

1. What is a word of wisdom?

2. What is a word of wisdom not?

3. Give some Bible examples of a word of wisdom.

4. Give some examples of a word of wisdom today. From your own life.

5. What are some of the ways a word of wisdom is received?

Chapter Five

WORD OF KNOWLEDGE

"To another the word of knowledge through the same Spirit." (1 Corinthians 12:8, NKJV)

WHAT IS THE GIFT OF A WORD OF KNOWLEDGE?

A word of knowledge is to know something you did not know in the natural. It's something God reveals to you. A word of knowledge deals with facts, to know something. A word of wisdom deals with action, to know what to do.

A word of knowledge does not make a person all-knowing and knowledgeable about everything. It's God giving someone knowledge for a specific situation for a specific moment in time.

WHAT THE GIFT OF A WORD OF KNOWLEDGE IS NOT

A word of knowledge is not suspicion (suspecting something). It's not intuition. It's not guessing something.

It's not finding out something through intelligence or research. It also has nothing to do with a person's inborn knowledge.

BIBLE EXAMPLES OF THE GIFT OF A WORD OF KNOWLEDGE

Jesus and the Samaritan Woman

In John chapter 4 we read about Jesus' encounter with the Samaritan woman at the well. Jesus asks her for a drink from the well and begins a conversation with her. Jesus tells her about the living water she can have. He then tells her to go get her husband and come back. She answers, "I have no husband." Jesus says,

> *"You have well said, 'I have no husband,' for you have had five husbands, and the one whom you now have is not your husband; in that you spoke truly.'"* (John 4:17-18, NKJV)

How did Jesus know that? It was through a word of knowledge.

Jesus and the Death of Lazarus

In John 11 we read where Lazarus was sick and his sisters, Mary and Martha, sent word to Jesus telling him of Lazarus' illness. The Bible says Jesus stayed where He was for two more days. After two days Jesus now starts the journey to where Lazarus is. Jesus tells His disciples,

> *"Our friend Lazarus has fallen asleep, but I am going there to wake him up."* (John 11:11, NIV)

"Lazarus is dead and for your sake I am glad I was not there, so that you may believe. But let us go to him." (John 11:14-15, NIV)

How did Jesus know that Lazarus was no longer sick, but was now dead? It was through a word of knowledge.

Jesus and Nathaniel

When Jesus called Nathaniel to follow Him the Bible says,

"Nathaniel said to Him, 'How do you know me?' Jesus answered him, 'Before Philip called you, when you were under the fig tree, I saw you.' " (John 1:48, ESV)

How did Jesus know Philip had been under a fig tree? It was through a word of knowledge.

Peter and Ananias and Sapphira

In Acts 5 we read where Ananias and Sapphira, members of the Early Church, sold a piece of property and from the proceeds gave money to the church. They said they gave all the money from the sale to the church, when in reality they kept some for themselves. The problem was not that they kept some of the money. They had every right to do so. The problem was they said they gave it all when they hadn't. When Peter confronts Ananias, he lies and says they gave it all. Peter says, "You have not lied to men but to God." The Bible says he fell down and died.

Three hours later, Ananias' wife, Sapphira, comes in, not knowing what has happened to her husband. Peter confronts her and she tells the same lie, that they gave it all, when in reality they had kept some of the money. She fell down and died.

How did Peter know they were lying and had kept back some of the money? Peter was not their accountant or banker. God gave Peter a word of knowledge.

Ananias Knew Where Saul Was Praying

In Acts 9 we read where God told Ananias (not the same Ananias as the one in Acts 5) that Saul (who later became Paul) was in a certain place praying.

"And the Lord said to him, 'Rise and go to the street called Straight, and at the house of Judas look for a man of Tarsus named Saul, for behold, he is praying.' " (Acts 9:11, ESV)

The only way Ananias could have known this was through a word of knowledge.

Peter Knew Three Men Were Looking for Him

In Acts 10 we read where the Holy Spirit told Peter that three men had arrived and were looking for him.

"And while Peter was pondering the vision, the Spirit said to him, 'Behold, three men are looking for you. Rise and go down and accompany them without hesitation, for I have sent them.' " (Acts 10:19-20, ESV)

The Holy Spirit gave Peter a word of knowledge.

EXAMPLES TODAY OF THE GIFT OF A WORD OF KNOWLEDGE

Man Gave Encouragement to a Fellow Passenger

I recently came across this testimony regarding a passenger giving a fellow passenger encouragement through a word of knowledge. There was no information regarding who it was, but the testimony read as follows.

"I was sitting next to a man on a flight to Australia and struck up a conversation with him and found him to be very engaging, even though he seemed a little distracted. We talked about life and family and careers. He was working for oil companies, and this was his last month traveling the globe for them. He was particularly fascinated by our work against human trafficking and was very touched. At one point he got up from his seat, and that's when I heard the voice of the Holy Spirit say to me, "I want you to encourage him about his retirement, which is coming fast."

I also heard a word of knowledge and got his wife's name; the place he always wanted to visit in Europe in his retirement; and knowledge about his daughter, who was pregnant with complications.

I was so overwhelmed that when he got back, I didn't know what to say, so I asked him if I could share with him some things I felt God was showing me in order to encourage him. He was very excited and said, yes. 'He told me your wife's name is Patricia. He also told me that He wants what you want more than you ever wanted it—like going to the Italian vineyards in southern Italy when you retire. He also told me about your daughter, Anna, and how she is pregnant but experiencing difficulties, and how you prayed and asked Him to help her. You told Him you would do anything if He would just help her. He wants to help her more than you do, and she and her baby are going to be okay.' He had tears in his eyes the whole time, and when I talked about his daughter, tears streamed down his face. He was gripping both seat handles intensely. When I finished I asked him if he felt this word was from God. 'Yes, all of it!' he said.

We prayed together and exchanged information. When I was at baggage claim I felt a hand on my shoulder. I turned around and it was my new friend. 'I can't believe God showed you all that. That was amazing! I feel like everything is right again in my world.'

Receiving just a one-minute bit of revelation from the Lord can be so powerful."[1]

God Warned Me I Was Going to Get Hit with a Golf Ball

We were holding services at a church in Wisconsin, and in the afternoon I went for a prayer walk as I usually do. As I walked on the outskirts of town I ended up walking on the outer perimeter of a golf course. As I was walking, there were two young men getting ready to tee off. As I looked in their direction, the Lord gave me a word of knowledge, saying, "You're going to get hit." I thought, *That can't be.* They were a good distance away and not pointed directly at me, but I thought I'd better keep an eye on them. As I'm looking in their direction, the first man hit the ball in the direction he was facing. I thought, *That's not going to hit me.* Suddenly the ball began to curve in my direction. I still was thinking, *It's going to miss me,* when suddenly it came directly toward me and I realized it was going to hit me. The ball hit me in my right thigh and fell to the ground. The men ran over to me, apologizing profusely and asking if I was all right. I told them I was fine. The next morning, however, I had a very black-and-blue thigh. If I had not received that word of knowledge, however, I possibly would have paid no attention to the golfers and would not have been looking and could possibly have been hit in the head, which would have been much more serious than being hit in the thigh.

God Showed Me Who I Would Marry

After graduating with a degree in marketing from Northern Michigan University in Marquette, MI, I was hired by the Woolworth company to work in management. The first store they assigned me to was in Stevens Point, WI. Upon arriving in town in May, I began attending the local Assemblies of God church. That summer the pastor started an early morning prayer meeting where people would meet at the church and pray on their way to work. There were about a half dozen of us who met at the church and we would spread out across the church sanctuary and pray by ourselves.

One morning as I was praying, the Lord gave me a word of knowledge through a vision. As I was praying, I received a vision of a lady holding a child in the nursery and I knew it was my wife and child, but I couldn't tell who it was; it was all blurry. Also, I was single and not dating anyone at this time. Suddenly the vision focused in like a telescope would focus in when you adjust it. The vision became clear and I saw it was Beth.

At this point we had never dated. We knew each other but had not shown any romantic interest in each other.

As the vision focused in, I thought, *This is crazy*. I thought perhaps the others at the prayer meeting were doing something. I opened my eyes and looked around. They were all busy praying.

I went back to prayer and the vision came back exactly the same way a second time; first blurry and then focused in clear. I again opened my eyes and looked around and everyone was praying. I went back to prayer and the vision came back a third time exactly like the first two times. I said, "Lord, if that's You, then You bring it to pass." Then I kind of forgot about it.

That was in July. In October we began dating. In February we were engaged. In August we were married, and as of this writing, we have been married for forty-three years.

God gave me a word of knowledge through a vision as to whom I was going to marry. By the way, I never told Beth about the vision until just before we were married. I didn't want her to feel like she had to do this because God said it, but I wanted it to be something she decided on her own between her and God.

A Key to Reaching Someone for Christ

Jackie Pullinger shared this testimony about how a word of knowledge was a key to helping her lead an old, lifelong Buddhist woman to Christ. Jackie was a missionary to Hong Kong and there was an old Buddhist woman she was trying to bring to Christ but she wasn't having any success. One day Jackie decided to begin to pray in the Holy Spirit for that old Buddhist lady. She would call out the lady's name and then pray for her in her prayer language. One day, when praying in the Spirit for her, the word "vegetable" came to mind. She thought that was strange, and decided to go ask that woman's son if the word "vegetable" would mean anything to his mother. The son said, "Oh, yes; my mother has only eaten vegetables all her life in order to try to please her God." With that new revelation, Jackie went back to that old Buddhist woman and said, "I want to tell you that God loves you so much for trying to please Him all your life by eating vegetables, and He has sent me here today to introduce you to Him, and His name is Jesus."[2]

That day that old Buddhist woman gave her life to Jesus. What was the key? It was the revelation of the word "vegetables." A word of knowledge: to know something you would have no way of knowing unless God showed it to you.

This illustrates how a word of knowledge can be instrumental in leading someone to Christ. "When we (*people*) are convinced that God truly knows us (*them*), we (*they*) can more readily surrender to His awesome will."[3]

Revelation of a Need of Healing

Another very common example of a word of knowledge in action today is God revealing to someone a condition in need of ministry. For example, in a service the Lord may give someone a word of knowledge that there is someone there with pain in a specific part of their body and God wants to minister to them.

The following testimony appeared in *Charisma* magazine. "While kneeling at the altar, Randy Clark felt a sharp pain in his left eye, lasting a split second. He had only recently received a 'crash course' in different ways to receive words of knowledge—downloads of supernatural information from the Holy Spirit that would otherwise be unknown to the recipient. One way is actually feeling the condition someone is experiencing.

Cautiously, the pastor of the small Midwestern church approached the pulpit microphone and stammered out, 'If…uh…some of you…uh, possibly has something wrong with your left eye, well…uh…if you just come forward, we'll pray for you.'

His confidence was diminutive and his faith was even smaller…gifts of the Spirit and healing miracles were foreign territory for this…pastor.

In a matter of minutes, a widow named Ruth approached the altar. Clark and his team gathered around her, praying until they ran out of things to say. That night, Ruth reportedly was healed of tunnel vision affecting her left eye.

The following Sunday, Clark gave the church an opportunity to share testimonies. A woman stood up in the back, and in a strong, Southern accent, said, 'Brother Randy, I think I'm having one of them there things you was just talking about, 'cause there's nothin' wrong with my right wrist, but it's killin' me.'

No one responded until the end of the church service. Then, right before the benediction, Clark's best friend's wife, Barbara, stood and addressed the congregation. With tears streaming down her face, she told of a debilitating pain in her wrists she had experienced for years. After two surgeries, and the insertion of plastic devices, she was about to give up hope. They prayed for her wrists and she was healed."[4]

Revelation of Sin in Order to Compassionately Minister

I don't remember where I heard this testimony of a man who was seated next to a man on a flight. During the course of the flight the Lord gave a word of knowledge that the man seated next to him was having an affair. The Lord showed him not only that the man was having an affair, but also gave the first name of the lady with whom he was having the affair.

The man lovingly spoke to the man having the affair, sharing what God had showed him. The man repented and accepted Christ.

If the man had not admitted to having an affair, repented, and given his life to Christ, this would not have necessarily meant that the word of knowledge was not accurate. Sometimes people will not accept the word of knowledge or respond.

I recall an incident in our second pastorate when God had given me a word of knowledge that there was someone in the service that night with pain in their stomach and God wanted to minister to them. When I shared that, no one responded, so we went on with the service. After the service, a lady came up to me in the lobby of the church and said, "That was me with the pain in my stomach. I was afraid to respond."

Keep in mind that just because there is not a response or if the response is not what we desired or expected, it doesn't mean we missed God and the word of knowledge was not accurate. Sometimes people don't respond as they should. Our part is to let God use us to give the word of knowledge. It is up to the recipient to respond.

Recipient of a Word of Knowledge from a Television Program

When Beth and I were in our first pastorate in Minnesota, we had just bought our first house. One day Beth got bit and scratched by a stray cat. We didn't know if the cat was rabid or had some other diseases. We asked our neighbor, who was a nurse, what we should do. She said to wash out the wounds with hydrogen peroxide and keep an eye on the wounds for signs of infection. We did as she suggested, but in the back of our minds we wondered about rabies and other diseases, knowing the long process and huge expenses if we got doctors involved.

One day right after this had happened, we "happened" to be watching *The 700 Club* on television. We usually didn't watch it because of our schedules, but that morning we "happened" to be watching. At the end of the telecast, Pat Robertson, the host of the program, was going to pray for those who were watching. Before praying, he had a word of knowledge. He said, "Someone is watching today. You've been bit by a cat and you are wondering and concerned that the cat was rabid and diseased. It is not; you will be fine."

We were stunned. That surely was not a normal kind of "word of knowledge" that he usually had. We accepted it as being from the Lord. In the coming days the wounds healed and Beth was fine.

A Word of Knowledge Regarding a Purchase

A word of knowledge can not only be helpful in ministry, and also in practical, everyday issues of life.

I remember hearing a testimony of a man needing to buy a car. He went out and found a car he really liked. It looked beautiful and was the kind of car he wanted. As he was getting ready to buy the car, he sensed a word of knowledge telling him the car had mechanical issues and to not buy the car. It had issues he could not see. The Lord was giving him a word of knowledge, giving him facts he would have no way of knowing unless God showed him.

He said he didn't listen to what God was trying to tell him and he bought the car anyway. He said the car was nothing but trouble. He should have listened to what God was trying to tell him.

A Word of Knowledge to Pray for Someone

Joni Jones shared the following testimony by an unnamed individual in a recent article in *Ministry Today* magazine entitled, "Holy Spirit Encounters."

"One night as I lay sleeping, the Spirit woke me up and said, 'Pray loudly for Frank'... I knew Frank, deployed overseas with the Army and living off-base, could easily be in danger... I rolled out of bed and went to the living room, alert and upset but unsure how to pray.

'Save my brother,' I pleaded with the Lord, pacing the floor in anguish.

The Spirit showed me an open vision of Frank, driving his little Mazda through dry, dense landscape on a bumpy dirt road, far from any town. The road, little more than two deep tire tracks, became a slippery, mess as he approached a wide, shallow stream.

Frank paused, analyzing whether his car could navigate eighteen inches of water. Sliding out of the car to investigate, he rested his hands on his hips, nodding his head as he pursed his lips, and surveyed the situation. On the other side of the stream and to his right grew a large strand of thin trees, whose thick leaves obscured the view.

'Pray he does not cross the stream,' the Spirit urged. 'Some locals are waiting to ambush, rob, and kill him.'

I finally understood the grave danger Frank faced. My prayers intensified. Now the Spirit showed me a scene laden with emotion. Upstream from my brother, another American soldier lay dead, half-in and half-out of the water. If he crossed the stream, Frank would face a similar fate.

Unable to escape the vision, I continued to pray.

Frank climbed into his car, turned it around, and slowly began his drive in the opposite direction. The vision ended, and I sighed in relief. God had saved my brother!

Later in the week, the phone rang at Frank's customary 5 a.m. time. He started to chat, but I interrupted him and described everything I remembered from my vision, not leaving anything out.

A long pause followed. 'The stream, turning around, it all happened just as you said,' he told me, stunned. 'But men weren't coming to ambush me,' he said. 'And no dead man lay upstream.'

'Oh, they'll find him soon,' I said, confident of the Holy Spirit's revelation.

A few days later, Frank called again, upset. 'They found the dead guy upstream, right where you said'."[5]

The Holy Spirit gave a word of knowledge through a vision, showing the need and what to pray.

HOW TO RECEIVE AND BE USED IN THE GIFT OF A WORD OF KNOWLEDGE

One of the ways a person can receive a word of knowledge is you sense in your inner being that these are the facts. It's something you sense. It's not suspicion or guessing, but something you sense.

Another way a person can receive a word of knowledge is through a vision or dream where God shows you through a vision or dream that these are the facts or this is the situation.

Still another way a person can receive a word of knowledge is through experiencing a brief pain in your body that is not the result of a problem you have yourself. Like in the Randy Clark testimony we shared earlier.

Upon receiving a word of knowledge, we then need to know what God would want us to do with it. In some situations He may have given it to us so we will know how to minister in that situation. For example, in a public setting He may want us to share it, like in the Randy Clark testimony. Or instead of stating it, He may want us to ask, "Is there someone here with…?" *(stating whatever He has shown us).*

In a one-on-one situation, perhaps in counseling someone or visiting with someone, a person can discretely ask, "Does this mean anything to you?" or, "I sense the Lord could be showing me this; does this mean anything to you?"

It's important to not only receive a word of knowledge, but also to know what to do with it. Some things are to be shared publicly, other things are to be shared privately, and still other things are just for you to know or for you to pray about but are not to be shared.

Upon receiving a word of knowledge, pray for wisdom as to what the Lord would want you to do with it.

REVIEW AND DISCUSSION QUESTIONS

1. What is a word of knowledge?

2. How does a word of knowledge differ from a word of wisdom?

3. What are some ways a person can receive a word of knowledge?

4. Give examples where perhaps you have received a word of knowledge.

5. Upon receiving a word of knowledge, what are some of the possible options of what to do with it?

Chapter Six

DISCERNING OF SPIRITS

"To another discerning of spirits." (1 Corinthians 12:10, NKJV)

WHAT IS THE GIFT OF THE DISCERNING OF SPIRITS?

The discerning of spirits is the Holy Spirit enabling us in a particular situation to distinguish whether something is of the Holy Spirit, of the human spirit, or of a satanic spirit. Some manifestations come from a human spirit, some from a demonic spirit, and some from the Holy Spirit. Is it of God, of Satan, or of the human spirit? This gift enables us to discern of what spirit it is. Both good and bad spirits inhabit the unseen world of spirits. This gift allows us to discern between good and evil spirits. "This gift is vital to keep a believer from being deceived."[1] This gift is God's answer to Satan's deception.[2]

WHAT THE GIFT OF THE DISCERNING OF SPIRITS IS NOT

The discerning of spirits is not some mystical, spooky gift. It's a very practical enablement from the Holy Spirit to discern if something is of God, Satan, or the human spirit. It's not guessing or assuming. It's not spiritual mind reading or psychological insight. "The gift of discerning of spirits is not a natural intuitive gift of showing good judgment or discernment."[3] "Discerning of spirits is not having remarkable insight, an aptitude for profound reasoning, or wise judgement."[4] It's not the power to discern the faults of others. Notice it is the discerning of *spirits*, not the gift of discernment. There is no gift of discernment; it is the gift of discerning of spirits. It's the discerning of the spirit behind someone or something, not natural discernment.

BIBLE EXAMPLES OF THE GIFT OF THE DISCERNING OF SPIRITS

Jesus Healing a Man Who Was Mute

In Luke 11:14 we read where Jesus healed a man who was mute. In this case the physical condition was the result of a demon.

> *"Jesus was driving out a demon that was mute. When the demon left, the man who had been mute spoke, and the crowd was amazed."* (Luke 11:14, NIV)

Jesus discerned that the physical condition was the result of a demon. Does this mean that all illness or physical problems are the result of a demon? Absolutley not! In fact, in most cases in Jesus' ministry and throughout the New Testament it was not. But, to honestly interpret Scripture, we must be aware of the fact that it is a possibility. The discerning of spirits will enable us to discern if the condition is just an illness or physical condition or the result of demonic activity.

Jesus Healing a Crippled Woman

In Luke 13:10-11 it says,

"On a Sabbath Jesus was teaching in one of the synagogues, and a woman was there who had been crippled by a spirit for eighteen years. She was bent over and could not straighten up at all." (Luke 13:10-11, NIV)

Notice her condition was the result of "a spirit." Does this mean that all people who are crippled or bent over have "a spirit" causing the condition? Absolutely not! Most are just crippled or bent over. But the possibility is that some physical conditions could be caused by "a spirit." The gift of discerning of spirits enables us to discern if they are.

The notes in the Fire Bible say, "Jesus sees some physical illness as the direct result of demonic activity or oppression. This crippled woman was troubled by 'a spirit'."[5]

Paul Delivering the Slave Girl

In Acts 16:16-18 we read where Paul and those who were with him were on their way to the place of prayer. Along the way they met a slave girl who had a spirit by which she predicted the future. She earned a great deal of money for her owners by fortune-telling. This girl followed Paul and his group, shouting, "These men are the servants of the Most High God, who are telling you the way to be saved." She kept this up for many days. Finally Paul became so troubled that he turned around and said to the spirit, "In the name of Jesus Christ, I command you to come out of her!" At that moment the spirit left her.

Notice what she was saying was correct, but Paul discerned through the gift of discerning of spirits that there was a spirit in her that was not of God.

Paul and Elymas

In Acts 13:6-12 we read where Paul, and those traveling with him, sailed to the island of Cyprus. As they traveled through the island they came to the city of Paphos. There they met a Jewish sorcerer and false prophet named Bar-Jesus, who was an attendant of the proconsul, Sergius Paulus.

The proconsul, an intelligent man, sent for Barnabas and Saul (Paul) because he wanted to hear the Word of God. But Elymas, the sorcerer (that is what his name means), opposed them and tried to turn the proconsul from the faith.

Then Paul, filled with the Holy Spirit, looked straight at Elymas and said,

> *"You are a child of the devil and an enemy of everything that is right! You are full of all kinds of deceit and trickery. Will you never stop perverting the right ways of the Lord? Now the hand of the Lord is against you. You are going to be blind, and for a time you will be unable to see the light of the sun. Immediately mist and darkness came over him, and he groped around looking for someone to lead*

him by the hand. When the proconsul saw what had happened, he became a believer." (Acts 13:10-12, NIV)

Through the gift of discerning of spirits, Paul discerned that the spirit that was in Elymas was not of God and not even of the flesh, but of the devil.

EXAMPLES TODAY OF THE GIFT OF THE DISCERNING OF SPIRITS

Discerning a "Word from the Lord"

Perhaps the most common area where the discerning of spirits comes into play today is to discern whether a "word from the Lord" was really a "word from the Lord" or not. This would be the case when a "word from the Lord" is given in a public service through one of the voice gifts, which we will cover in later chapters, or a person coming up to an individual and saying, "I have a word from the Lord for you," which we will also cover later in the book.

The Bible admonishes us in several places to not just accept "a word being from the Lord," but to discern whether it really is a word from the Lord. The Scripture admonishes us:

"Do not believe every spirit, but test the spirits to see whether they are from God, because many false prophets have gone out into the world." (1 John 4:1, NIV)

"Two or three prophets should speak, and the others should weigh carefully what is said." (1 Corinthians 14:29, NIV)

"Do not treat prophecies with contempt. Test everything. Hold on to the good." (1 Thessalonians 5:20-21, NIV)

The gift of discerning of spirits enables us to discern if a "word from the Lord" is really a "word from the Lord."

Discerning the Spirit of a Ministry

There was a time in our first pastorate when satellite dishes were first becoming popular. A ministry in Texas started broadcasting their programing into local churches that would purchase satellite dishes and sign up for their programing. Individuals began traveling the country, selling the satellite dishes and programing to churches and to individuals.

I remember being approached by a person selling the dishes and programing. As I listened to his presentation and thought about it later, there was a very unsettled, uneasy feeling about it. There was not a peace about it. Later when he contacted us to see if we wanted to get the equipment and sign up, I thanked him but said we weren't interested.

We later found out the salesperson had deceived and swindled individuals financially and had not come through with what he had promised. Also, later as time went on, it was exposed that the entire ministry was corrupt with lies and deception.

I was so thankful for the gift of discerning of spirits for that situation. That uneasy, unsettled feeling of the Holy Spirit saying, "Don't get involved," was the discerning of spirits.

When needed, the discerning of spirits enables us to know what is motivating a person. If it's not right, there will be a check in your spirit. The discerning of spirits is "God's alarm system for the Church."[6]

HOW TO RECEIVE AND BE USED IN THE GIFT OF THE DISCERNING OF SPIRITS

The obvious place to begin is to ask, "Is it scriptural?" Does the "word from the Lord" line up with Scripture? If the "word from the Lord," or whatever area we are in need of the discerning of spirits in, doesn't line up with Scripture, no further discernment is needed. The issue is settled. In fact, at this point, this really wouldn't even be the gift of discerning of spirits; this is just basic Bible application. It's at the next level that the gift is in operation.

After asking if it is scriptural, the next test would be, "What am I sensing?" Are we sensing the peace of God? Or is there an uneasy, unsettled feeling? Are we sensing this is God? Or are we sensing this is of the enemy? Or do we sense this is of the flesh?

After we have received this discernment, the question then becomes, "What do we do with this?" The answer would depend on the situation. In some cases, the discernment may only be for you to know. In other cases, what you are discerning needs to be shared either publicly or with others. We need to pray and ask God what to do. Not everything needs to be shared. On the other hand, some things need to be shared either publicly or with individuals.

REVIEW AND DISCUSSION QUESTIONS

1. Describe the gift of discerning of spirits.

2. What is not the discerning of spirits?

3. Give some Bible examples of discerning of spirits.

4. Give some examples of discerning of spirits from your life.

5. How is the gift of discerning of spirits received? What do we do with what we have discerned?

Chapter Seven

GIFT OF FAITH

"To another faith by the same Spirit." (1 Corinthians 12:9, NKJV)

WHAT IS THE GIFT OF FAITH?

The gift of faith is an extraordinary faith God gives for a specific purpose or situation. "The gift of faith is supernatural faith God gives to a person at a specific time and for a specific purpose."[1] When the gift of faith comes upon a person for a particular situation, they "just know" that things are going to "work out." When the gift of faith comes on an individual, the possibility of it not working out doesn't even seem like a possibility. It doesn't matter what the circumstances may look like. It doesn't matter what people are saying. It doesn't matter what the reports are. It's an extraordinary faith God gives for a particular situation.

WHAT THE GIFT OF FAITH IS NOT

The gift of faith is not hoping things will work out. It's not positive thinking. It's not stubbornness. It's not ordinary faith. "It's not planned or developed. The faith needed is just suddenly there."[2]

BIBLE EXAMPLES OF THE GIFT OF FAITH

Paul and the Shipwreck

In Acts 27:21-26 we read where Paul is being taken to Rome to stand trial against the false charges that were brought against him. Along the way the ship encounters a fierce storm with hurricane-force winds. For many days the storm continued to rage and all hope of surviving seemed lost.

Paul then stood up and said,

"Men, you should have taken my advice to not sail from Crete; then you would have spared yourselves this damage and loss. But now I urge you to keep up your courage, because not one of you will be lost; only the ship will be destroyed. Last night an angel of the God whose I am and whom I serve stood beside me and said, 'Do not be afraid, Paul. You must stand trial before Caesar; and God has graciously given you the lives of all who sail with you.' So keep up your courage, men, for I have faith in God that it will happen just as he told me. Nevertheless, we must run aground on some island." (Acts 27:21-26, NIV)

This would be an example of the gift of faith. Regardless of how the circumstances looked, Paul knew that they were going to survive. Later in Acts 27 we read where it turned out exactly as God said it would.

The gift of faith, an extraordinary faith God gives for a particular situation. In this case this gift was received through a word from an angel.

EXAMPLES TODAY OF THE GIFT OF FAITH

Smith Wigglesworth Testimony

I came across this testimony regarding Smith Wigglesworth, a great evangelist in the early 1900s.

The article said, one day when coming home from an open-air meeting, Wigglesworth learned that his wife, Polly, was at Mr. Mitchell's house. The day before when Wigglesworth had visited Mitchell, the sick man had been close to death. As Wigglesworth hurried to Mitchell's house, he heard screaming coming from the house. On the way into Mr. Mitchell's room, he passed Mrs. Mitchell, who was crying, "He's gone! He's gone!"

Wigglesworth related his experience:

"I just passed Mrs. Mitchell and went into the room and immediately I saw that Mitchell had gone. I could not understand it, but I began to pray. My wife was always afraid that I would go too far, and she laid hold of me and said, 'Don't, Dad! Don't you see that he is dead?' But I continued praying. I got as far as I could with my own faith, and then God laid hold of me. Oh, it was such a laying hold that I could believe for anything. The faith of the Lord Jesus laid hold of me and a solid peace came into my heart. I shouted, 'He lives! He lives! He lives!' And he is living today."[3]

This is an example of extraordinary faith for a particular situation.

Another Smith Wigglesworth Testimony

"They called Smith Wigglesworth one day and said, 'Brother Wigglesworth, would you come to the house and pray for Uncle Fred? He's dying.' He said, 'I'll come; just not now.'

They called him again and said, 'Please, you've got to come! He's in a bad way. He's dying!'

Wigglesworth said, 'I told you, I'll come in a little while.'

They called him back a few minutes later and said, 'Don't bother. Uncle Fred is dead.'

Wigglesworth said, 'I'm coming.'

When Wigglesworth arrived, he found Uncle Fred dead and already in his coffin. There were about sixty mourners in the room. Wigglesworth walked right up to the coffin, yanked the corpse out of it, pushed the body up against the wall, and said, 'Walk, in the name of Jesus!' The corpse fell to the floor.

Wigglesworth just bent down, picked it up, and stood it against the wall again. He commanded, 'Walk, in the name of Jesus!' The corpse fell to the floor again.

But Wigglesworth didn't stop. He bent down, picked the corpse up again, slammed it against the wall, and thundered, 'I told you to walk!' And the man walked!

Wigglesworth turned and calmly walked out the door.

It was not his faith; it was the gift of faith. When the gift of faith comes on you, you don't take no for an answer."[4]

Our Going to Our First Pastorate

As we were approaching the time of my graduating from North Central Bible College (now North Central University), we sensed God calling us to go directly into pastoring a church. Since North Central Bible College was located in Minnesota, I figured the place to begin looking for a pastorate was in Minnesota, so I went in to talk to the district superintendent.

He told me of a church in west central Minnesota that was looking for a pastor. He told me it was a small town of about 750 people and then he told me about the church. He called it "a wonderful opportunity." I have now learned what it means when a superintendent calls a church "a wonderful opportunity." What he means is he can't find anybody to go there and he wishes you would go there.

I learned it was such "a great opportunity" that two years earlier the district office had closed the church. After they had closed the church, one of the former pastors was retiring and moving back to town. He felt bad that a church he had previously pastored was now closed, so he asked the district office if he could reopen the church. They agreed and he began holding services. A small group of people began attending and then the pastor had a heart attack and the doctor said, "You can't pastor anymore." Now the district officials needed to find a new pastor for this "wonderful opportunity."

We found out that many pastors had come and gone over the years. We also found out some things had happened that were not good things to have happened in a church, especially in a small town where news travels fast. We were told the salary would be fifty dollars a week and the parsonage would be an apartment attached to the church building. Also, at this time Beth was pregnant, expecting our first child.

Nothing in common sense said to pursue this "wonderful opportunity" except God put it on our hearts to pursue it.

We arranged to go there on an Easter Sunday to preach and meet the people of the church. After that Sunday they had a business meeting and voted us in as their new pastor. We were so excited. We hadn't even graduated from Bible college yet and we already had our first pastorate. The plan was that we would finish our last month of Bible college and right after graduation we would move and begin pastoring the church.

We were so excited! But when we told others who knew the church and its history, they thought we were crazy to go there. They wondered if we knew what we were doing.

We began to wonder, *What have we done, what have we gotten ourselves into, what's going to happen to us?*

But I believe at that time God gave us a gift of faith for that situation and we just knew that it was going to work out. It didn't matter what the past history was. It didn't matter what people were saying. We just knew that we knew that it was going to work out. It was a gift of faith for a particular situation.

Later in the book (*because it involves two other gifts of the Holy Spirit*) we'll tell what helped to bring about that gift of faith, and we'll also tell what God did and how it all worked out.

HOW TO RECEIVE A GIFT OF FAITH

Perhaps the most common way a gift of faith is received is that you just sense an extraordinary faith for a particular situation. You just know what the outcome will be regardless of the odds, the reports, or what the present situation may look like.

Also, there may be times where that gift of faith may be given or fueled by something from God. For example, in the account of Paul and the shipwreck that we described earlier, an angel appeared to Paul and told him no lives would be lost in spite of the horrific storm.

In the illustration we shared earlier about our going to our first pastorate, there were two other gifts of the Holy Spirit that were involved which we will describe later.

In any case, the end result is an extraordinary faith for a particular situation. Upon receiving a gift of faith, the question then becomes, "What do I do with it?" The answer would depend on the situation. There are times when the gift is meant to be shared, as in the case of Paul and those on the ship. An example today would be in a meeting (*whether in a group or one-on-one*) where a difficult situation is being faced and someone receives a gift of faith. Sharing it would be greatly encouraging to those you are with.

On the other hand, it may be a personal situation, and the gift of faith is meant just for you in your situation. The situation and circumstances and what the Holy Spirit is saying to you will determine whether it should be shared or is meant just for you.

REVIEW AND DISCUSSION QUESTIONS

1. Describe what the gift of faith is.

2. Describe what the gift of faith is not.

3. Can you think of some other examples of the gift of faith in action today?

4. How is a gift of faith received?

5. What should you do when you receive a gift of faith?

Chapter Eight

GIFTS OF HEALINGS

"To another gifts of healings." (1 Corinthians 12:9, NKJV)

WHAT ARE THE GIFTS OF HEALINGS?

The gifts of healings are to supernaturally give healing to someone in Jesus' name. To pronounce someone healed in Jesus' name. "The gift of healing is not for the one who ministers the gift. The gift is for the sick person—the one who receives the gift."[1]

Over the years there have been cases where people have pronounced everyone healed or pronounced individuals healed when they were not. This was not the gifts of healings in operation. I remember a Bible college professor telling us this gift never fails. Where this gift is in operation, the individual is always healed. If they are not healed, this gift was not in operation. There are no Bible examples where this gift was in operation and the individual was not healed.

Just because there have been misguided individuals or abuses does not negate the fact that there is a legitimate gift.

Notice both "gifts" and "healings" are plural in the Greek, the original language in which most of the New Testament was written. A brochure on the gifts of the Holy Spirit published by the Assemblies of God states, "There is not one 'gift of healing' but many to meet all kinds of sickness and disease, even in the same service or setting."[2]

Also, this gift can be manifested in a variety of ways. In John 9:6-7, there was a man who had been blind from birth. Jesus spit on the ground, made mud with the saliva, and put it on the man's eyes.

"He spit on the ground, made some mud with the saliva, put it on the man's eyes. 'Go,' He told him, 'wash in the Pool of Siloam'... So the man went and washed, and came home seeing." (John 9:6-7, NIV)

There were other times in Jesus' ministry where He touched people and sometimes He just used words to pronounce healing.

WHAT THE GIFTS OF HEALINGS ARE NOT

This gift is not prayer for the sick. This gift is not anointing the sick with oil. This gift is not asking God to heal someone. These are all things we need to do. The Bible says,

"Is any one of you sick? He should call the elders of the church to pray over him and anoint him with oil in the name of the Lord. And the prayer offered

in faith will make the sick person well; the Lord will raise him up." (James 5:14-15, NIV)

We need to pray for the sick as the Scripture says and that can lead to the gift of healing being manifested, but prayer for the sick is not the gift of healing in operation.

BIBLE EXAMPLES OF THE GIFTS OF HEALINGS

Peter and John and the Lame Man

We find an example of the gift of healing in operation in Acts 3:1-10. It's three o'clock in the afternoon and Peter and John are on their way to the temple to pray when they encounter a lame man being carried to the temple gate. He had been crippled from birth and put there every day to beg from those going to the temple. When the lame man saw Peter and John about to enter the temple, he asked them for money.

Peter looked at him and said, "Look at us!" The man looked at them, expecting to get some money. Then Peter said,

"Silver or gold I do not have, but what I have I give you. In the name of Jesus Christ of Nazareth, walk." (Acts 3:6, NIV)

Peter took him by the right hand and helped him up and instantly the man's feet and ankles became strong and he began to walk. He went into the temple courts with Peter and John, walking and jumping, and praising God.

Notice the pronouncement of healing. "What I have I give you." The Holy Spirit was giving Peter a specific gift of healing to give to the lame man. As we said earlier, the gift of healing is not for the one who ministers the gift; it is for the sick person — the one who receives the gift.

Also, the Spirit did not give Peter a permanent gift of healing. He had to receive a new gift of healing from the Holy Spirit each time the gift was going to be manifested. As with all the gifts, we don't own or possess the gifts, but they are used at a specific time for a specific situation.

Also, notice in this case, Peter did not even pray for the lame man. He just simply gave the lame man a gift that the Holy Spirit had given him at that moment to give to the lame man.

Jesus' Ministry

As we look at Jesus' ministry in the Gospels we notice how at times Jesus simply pronounced healing to sick individuals. He gave them a gift of healing and then told them to go have it confirmed.

For example, in Luke 17:11-19 when Jesus was met by ten lepers who cried out to Him to have mercy on them, the Bible says,

> *"When he saw them he said to them, 'Go and show yourselves to the priests.' And as they went they were cleansed."* (Luke 17:14, ESV)

There is no mention of Jesus even praying for them. He simply gave them the gift of healing and told them to show themselves to the priests to have it confirmed (back then the priests had the authority to pronounce someone cleansed of leprosy).

Another example in Jesus' ministry is found in John 5:2-9. In this account Jesus encounters a man who had been an invalid for thirty-eight years. Jesus asked him if he wanted to be healed. In verse 8 we read,

"Jesus said to him, 'Get up, take up your bed, and walk.' And at once the man was healed, and he took up his bed and walked." (John 5:8-9, ESV)

There is no mention of Jesus even praying for the man. He simply gave him the gift of healing.

EXAMPLES OF THE GIFTS OF HEALINGS TODAY

I recall teaching this at a "Gifts of the Holy Spirit Seminar" at a church, where during the question-and-answer time, a lady raised her hand to ask a question. She said recently she had been visiting her dad in the hospital. As she was praying for him, she sensed the Holy Spirit saying he was healed and she told him, "Dad, you're healed." She asked, "Was that the gift of healing?" I said, "Yes."

HOW TO BE USED IN THE GIFTS OF HEALINGS

The best way to be available to be used in the gift of healing is to pray for the sick. A person can be used without any prayer being involved, as in the case of Peter and John and the lame man, but more often than not, this gift will flow out of praying for the sick.

Also, "sometimes the person ministering the gift of healing will tell the person in need to do certain things; of course, this is always a Spirit-directed action."[3] Some examples from Jesus ministry would be:

In Mark 3:5 (ESV) Jesus said to the man with the withered hand, "Stretch out your hand." He stretched it out, and his hand was restored.

In Mark 2:4-11(ESV) Jesus said to the paralytic, "I say to you, rise, pick up your bed, and go home." He rose and immediately picked up his bed and went out before them all.

As we are praying for the sick, be open to the prompting of the Holy Spirit. If the Holy Spirit is telling you they are healed, then declare it to them and tell them to have it confirmed with their doctor.

REVIEW AND DISCUSSION QUESTIONS

1. Describe what the gifts of healings is.

2. Describe what the gifts of healings is not.

3. Why are the words "gifts" and "healings" plural?

4. What is the best way to position ourselves to be used in the gifts of healings?

5. Why have the recipient of the gift of healing confirm it with a doctor?

Chapter Nine

WORKING OF MIRACLES

"To another the working of miracles." (1 Corinthians 12:10, NKJV)

WHAT IS THE GIFT OF WORKING OF MIRACLES?

The working of miracles is the divine counteracting of the normal forces or laws of nature. "Miracles transcend natural law."[1]

This can include spiritual deliverance from demonic forces; physical deliverance in ominous, life-threatening situations; a positive change for favor in the midst of difficult situations; and timely provisions for human need.

WHAT THE GIFT OF THE WORKING OF MIRACLES IS NOT

The working of miracles is not hoping something will happen or work out. It's not guessing that something will happen, nor is it something that would just normally happen.

BIBLE EXAMPLES OF THE GIFT OF WORKING OF MIRACLES

Jesus' Ministry

Some examples from Jesus' ministry would be:

- Jesus turning water into wine (John 2:9)

- Jesus raising the widow's son from the dead (Luke 7:11)

- Jesus feeding the five thousand (Matthew 14:15)

- Jesus walking on the water (Matthew 14:25)

- Jesus stopping the storm (Matthew 8:26)

Not only did Jesus perform miracles to relieve the needs and suffering of people, but He also illustrated God's power to forgive sin with demonstrations of His power. Miracles validated the Gospel message and truth of God's Word.[2]

Peter Raising Dorcas from the Dead

In Acts 9:36-43 we read where Dorcas became sick and died. Her body was washed and brought to an upstairs room.

When the disciples heard that Peter was in the neighboring town of Lydda, they sent two men to get him. When Peter arrived, he was brought upstairs to where Dorcas lay. Peter sent all the mourners out of the room and got down on his knees and prayed. Turning toward the dead woman, Peter said,

" *'Tabitha (when translated is Dorcas)*, **get up.'** " (Acts 9:40, NIV)

She opened her eyes, and seeing Peter, she sat up. Peter took her by the hand and helped her to her feet. He then called all those who were at the house and presented her to them alive.

Peter's Miraculous Escape from Prison

In Acts 12 we read where King Herod had executed James, one of the leaders of the Early Church. When Herod saw that this pleased the Jews, he had Peter arrested and was going to execute him after the Passover.

He had Peter kept in prison until the upcoming trial and execution. Meanwhile the church was praying for Peter.

The night before the trial, Peter, bound with two chains, was sleeping between two soldiers and sentries who stood guard at the entrance to the prison.

Suddenly an angel of the Lord appeared, struck Peter on the side, and woke him up, saying, "Quick, get up!" The chains fell off Peter's wrists. The angel then said, "Put on your clothes and sandals… Wrap your cloak around you and follow me."

Peter followed him out of the prison. They passed the first and second guards and then came to the iron gate leading to the city. The gate opened for them by itself and they walked out of the prison.

After they had walked the length of one street, suddenly the angel left him.

EXAMPLES OF THE WORKING
OF MIRACLES TODAY

Pastor in Vietnam

I remember reading the testimony of a pastor in Vietnam. He was pastoring a church in his village, but no one seemed to be interested in his message about Jesus.

One day a husband and wife came to his office and asked him to come and pray for their son. The pastor agreed and followed them to their home. When they arrived, the pastor was stunned. He thought they were asking him to come and pray for their son who was sick. When he arrived, he immediately saw the boy was not sick; he was dead!

The pastor later said he was so shaken, he didn't even remember what he prayed. But he prayed and left.

The next morning the pastor was in his office and there was a knock on the door. The pastor said, "Come in." The door opened and there was the husband and wife. And behind them was their son! He was alive! Raised from the dead!

After that, as news spread throughout the village, it seemed everybody wanted to hear about Jesus.

Man Delivered from a Snake in Africa

"As Nemgistu was telling a group of men in Africa about Jesus, a snake slithered noiselessly through the grass toward the men. As Nemgistu was talking, he was completely unaware of the snake's presence.

By the time he noticed the snake, it had coiled three times around one of his legs and was stretching toward the other leg. The audience of some thirty men watched in horror. They knew the viper's technique of wrapping itself around the victim's legs to bring him to the ground.

Nemgistu paused only momentarily in his message. Looking down at his attacker, he said, 'In the name of Jesus, go!'

To the astonishment of the men, the snake immediately uncoiled and disappeared into the grass. Nemgistu continued his message about Jesus, and every man listened. The demonstration of the miraculous power in the Name of Jesus had captivated them!"[3]

Crop Miraculously Spared

"Many Miao (Hmong) people in Northern Asia are Christians. Most live simply, making a living from agriculture on the high, arid slopes around their tiny villages.

One village of Christian Miao invested in mulberry trees, the leaves of which are used in the summer to feed silkworms. It can be a profitable investment — if the leaves mature.

One day in late spring, someone noticed caterpillars eating the mulberry leaves. Soon the caterpillars were everywhere. Men, women, even children were sent to pick the caterpillars from the trees. They worked as fast as they could, but their efforts failed to make a dent in the number of caterpillars. Eventually the workers stopped because pulling the branches was destroying the young leaves.

Pesticides could have helped, but none was available within a few days' walk. Even then, the Miao didn't have the money to make such a purchase. The situation looked hopeless.

'Let's go to church,' one believer suggested. 'Our efforts are useless. Let's call out to God…'

Everyone agreed. They made their way to the church, and with voices as one, called out to God for help. They didn't return to their homes until late that night.

Early the next morning, as one of the believers aroused himself to return to the church, he heard the cawing of a crow. Looking into the still-gray sky, he could see a large flock of birds circling overhead. Suddenly the birds swooped down on the mulberry grove and began feeding on the fat caterpillars.

The Miao believers watched from the village as the crows feasted all day. Then just before evening, the birds left, never to be seen again. And in the mulberry grove, not one living caterpillar could be found.

The leaves were harvested later that summer and the Miao's yearly cash crop was saved. They knew God had heard their prayers and had done a miracle."[4]

Car Kept on an Icy Road

I remember a spring evening when I was a student at Northern Michigan University in Marquette, MI, about 140 miles from my hometown. I had gone home for the weekend and was driving back to the university. I had some fellow students with me and we were enjoying one another's company on the trip back to college when suddenly the road became very icy.

Suddenly the car began to fishtail on the icy road, first one way, then the other way, each time the back end of the car going further and further. It seemed like the inevitable result would be the car would spin completely around one or more times and hopefully no oncoming traffic would be coming.

I was praying for God to help us when suddenly it was as if an angel put their hands on the back of the car and said, "Stay." The fishtailing suddenly stopped, the car straightened out, and we safely arrived at our destination.

There was no logical reason for what had happened. Except God had done a miracle!

Car Not Hitting a Deer

Beth and I were in our second pastorate. It was an early December evening in Wisconsin and we were on our way to our sectional ministers' and spouses' Christmas party in a neighboring community.

As we were driving, suddenly without warning, a herd of about eight to twelve deer (I didn't stop to count them) starting running across the road right in front of us. There was no time to do anything but quickly pray, slow down, close our eyes (in case of shattering glass), hold tight to the steering wheel, and brace ourselves for impact.

The impact never came! The next thing we knew, we were on the other side of where the deer had run across the road. There was no way we could have missed that many deer running right in front of us. God had done a miracle!

HOW TO BE USED IN THE GIFT OF WORKING OF MIRACLES

Seeing the working of miracles begins by being open to the leading of the Holy Spirit. When you see the need for a miracle, then pray and ask God to do a miracle.

If we don't see the need for a miracle or don't pray and ask God for a miracle, we won't see God do miracles.

It's great to hear testimonies of miracles, but even greater to be a part of a miracle! Pray for a miracle when one is needed.

REVIEW AND DISCUSSION QUESTIONS

1. Describe what the gift of the working of miracles is.

2. Describe what the gift of the working of miracles is not.

3. What are some examples of the working of miracles in the Bible?

4. What are some miracles that have happened in your life?

5. How can we position ourselves to see the gift of miracles in or through our life?

Chapter Ten

PROPHECY

&

"To another prophecy." (1 Corinthians 12:10, NKJV)

WHAT IS THE GIFT OF PROPHECY?

The gift of prophecy is to speak a message from God in a language known to the speaker. The message can be either forthtelling (giving a message from God) or it can also be foretelling (telling what will happen).

The purpose of the gift of prophecy is found in 1 Corinthians 14:3-4,

"But everyone who prophesies speaks to men for their strengthening, encouragement and comfort... he who prophesies edifies the church." (1 Corinthians 14:3-4 ,NIV)

The New King James Version of 1 Corinthians 14:3-4 says,

"But he who prophesies speaks edification and exhortation and comfort ... he who prophesies edifies the church."

Edification means "to build up." Exhortation means "to call near," "to urge forward," "to admonish," and "to appeal."

The purpose of the gift of prophecy is to strengthen, encourage, comfort, and edify the church. The purpose is not to destroy, discourage, or tear down.

A word of prophecy may at times be confrontational or convicting, but will always be done in a spirit of love and will always be for the ultimate purpose of building up.

An example would be found in 2 Samuel 12. After David had committed adultery with Uriah's wife, Bathsheba, and then arranged to have Uriah killed, God sent Nathan with a message for David. The message confronted David regarding what he had done, but it was done in a spirit of love and for the purpose of urging David to confess and repent of his sin. The message was not to destroy, discourage, or tear down David, but to exhort David (admonish and appeal to David) to confess and repent of his sin.

Paul wrote this regarding a word of prophecy given in a public church setting, but it could also be applied to a one-on-one personal setting,

"But if all prophesy, and an unbeliever or outsider enters, he is convicted by all, he is called to account by all, the secrets of his heart are disclosed, and so falling on his face, he will worship God and declare

that God is really among you." (1 Corinthians 14:24-25, ESV)

A word of prophecy can be given in a public church setting for the church, which is the context of Paul's writing in 1 Corinthians 12 and 14. When given in a public service, individuals can then sense the Holy Spirit applying it to their individual lives and situations or to the entire church.

On the other hand, a word of prophecy can also be given for an individual, as in the case of Agabus giving a word of prophecy for Paul in Acts 21,

"A prophet named Agabus came down from Judea. Coming over to us, he took Paul's belt, tied his own hands and feet with it and said, 'In this way the Jews of Jerusalem will bind the owner of this belt and turn him over to the Gentiles.' " (Acts 21:10-11, NIV)

A word of prophecy for an individual is not given for the purpose of ruling or directing but rather to confirm what God has already been saying to the individual. The implication from the wording of Paul's response to Agabus' word of prophecy is that Paul already sensed he was ready to be bound and even die in Jerusalem.

"Then Paul answered, 'What are you doing, weeping and breaking my heart? For I am ready not only to be imprisoned but even to die in Jerusalem for the name of the Lord Jesus.' " (Acts 21:13, ESV)

By the way, Paul did not disobey the word of prophecy by going to Jerusalem. The word of prophecy didn't tell him not to go, but rather told him what would happen to him when he went, confirming what he already sensed.

Charles Crabtree said in his book, *The Pentecostal Priority*, "Thousands have been devastated by the unscriptural practice of giving personal prophecies as directives rather than as confirmations."[1]

"Personal prophecy must never guide you. Prophecy must confirm what you already know in your heart."[2]

Regarding receiving a personal word of prophecy from someone, Jack Hayford gives the following sound advice in his notes in the *Spirit-Filled Life Bible*.

1. The word will not be new to the mind of the one addressed.

   "And now, behold, I am going to Jerusalem, constrained by the Spirit, not knowing what will happen to me there, except that the Holy Spirit testifies to me in every city that imprisonment and afflictions await me. But I do not account my life of any value nor as precious to myself, if only I may finish my course and the ministry that I received from the Lord Jesus to testify to the gospel of the grace of God." (Acts 20:22-24, ESV)

2. The character of the one giving the word should be weighed.

   "And one of them named Agabus stood up and foretold by the Spirit that there would be a great famine over all the world (this took place in the days of Claudius)." (Acts 11:28, ESV)

"While we were staying for many days, a prophet named Agabus came down from Judea." (Acts 21:10, ESV)

3. The prophecy is not to be controlling. Paul did not change his plans (Acts 21:14).

   "And since he would not be persuaded, we ceased and said, 'Let the will of the Lord be done.' " (Acts 21:14, ESV)

4. The prophecy is in part and does not give us the whole picture.

   "For we know in part and we prophesy in part." (1 Corinthians 13:9, ESV)

5. We should prayerfully consider the word as Mary did.

   "But Mary treasured up all these things, pondering them in her heart." (Luke 2:19, ESV)

   First Thessalonians 5:20-21 says,

   "Do not treat prophesies with contempt. Test everything. Hold on to the good." (1 Thessalonians 5:20-21, NIV)[3]

WHAT THE GIFT OF PROPHECY IS NOT

Giving a word of prophecy is not you saying in the natural what you think needs to be said. Also, the gift of prophecy is not knowing end-time events, nor is it ordinary preaching. It's God giving you a message by His Holy Spirit to share with the church or even with an individual at a specific time and situation.

Giving a word of prophecy is not the same as being called to be a prophet. Giving a word of prophecy does not make a person a prophet as listed in Ephesians 4:11. What is listed in Ephesians 4 is a calling, not a gift of the Holy Spirit. Agabus was a prophet by calling but in the case mentioned previously was being given a word of prophecy regarding Paul.

BIBLE EXAMPLES OF THE GIFT OF PROPHECY

As we look through the New Testament, we find several examples of how the gift of prophecy was part of the life of the Early Church.

In Acts 21:8 we read about Philip's daughters who prophesied,

"We reached Caesarea and stayed at the house of Philip the evangelist... He had four unmarried daughters who prophesied." (Acts 21:8-9, NIV)

In 1 Thessalonians 5:20 we read,

"Do not treat prophecies with contempt." (1 Thessalonians 5:20, NIV)

In 1 Corinthians 14:1 Paul writes,

"Eagerly desire spiritual gifts, especially the gift of prophecy." (1 Corinthians 14:1, NIV)

In 1 Corinthians 14:39, Paul encourages the believers in Corinth regarding prophecy by writing,

"Therefore, my brothers, be eager to prophesy... but everything should be done in a fitting and orderly way." (1 Corinthians 14:39-40, NIV)

We also find examples of personal prophecy in the life of the Early Church. Some examples are:

Agabus prophesying to Paul what awaited him in Jerusalem,

"He took Paul's belt, tied his own hands and feet with it and said, 'In this way the Jews of Jerusalem will bind the owner of this belt and hand him over to the Gentiles.' " (Acts 21:11, NIV)

In 1 Timothy 1:18, Paul encourages Timothy to not forget the prophecies that were given over him,

"Timothy, my son, I give you this instruction in keeping with the prophecies once made about you." (1 Timothy 1:18, NIV)

Paul reminding Timothy in 1 Timothy 4:14,

"Do not neglect your gift, which was given you through a prophetic message when the body of elders laid their hands on you." (1 Timothy 4:14, NIV)

EXAMPLES OF THE GIFT OF PROPHECY TODAY

An example of the gift of prophecy in operation today would be a person, under the inspiration and direction of the Holy Spirit, speaking out a message of edification, exhortation, or comfort at an appropriate time in a public service.

Another example, especially in churches with large sanctuaries, or perhaps where there have been issues with unscriptural messages being given by individuals, would be the policy of having the person go to one of the pastors or designated leaders and sharing the gist of their word of prophecy to the pastor or designated leader for approval and then going to a microphone to give it so everyone can hear it, or having the leader share it from a microphone on their behalf. In some cases the person may write it down and show it to one of those designated for approval and then go to a microphone to share it if it has been approved.

Pastor Jeff Leake, pastor of a large church in Allison Park, PA, wrote this interesting insight in his book, *Power for Life*.

"The world has changed since 1906 and Azuza Street, when people gathered for worship on the top floor of an old hall with sawdust floors, wooden benches, and no electronic sound systems. The practice was for a person to stand up in the service, take the floor, and declare a word from God. That was the culture of the day before sound systems, stages, etc. Town hall meetings and small country venues were the order of the day. Today someone shouting out a message can seem so unusual and unsettling in our culture. In their church in Allison Park, when someone feels they have a word of prophecy, instead of shouting from their seats, they come to one of the pastoral team members and share with them what they are sensing. If the pastoral team member senses it is from God, they then have that individual come up on the platform to share the message or one the pastoral team member will share it on their behalf. Pastor Leake says this one change has done more to make everyone feel safe than anything else. This also has led to several other things: (1) quiet and shy people who would never have shouted from the back are being used in spiritual gifts, (2) people who attend our church feel safe and are bringing their friends to church in greater numbers, (3) we are teaching how to use the gifts in a normal tone and an explained fashion, and (4) more people are using spiritual gifts in their everyday lives."[4]

Dr. James Bradford shared this experience of when he became pastor of Central Assembly, a large church in Springfield, MO. Since it was such a large church, he thought it only natural to let the church know that if they had a word from the Lord they had microphones set up for them to use. Otherwise, there was no way everyone could hear the message in such a large auditorium. He also let the church know he was available at the front to talk to individuals if they were not sure if their message was from God. He said he also discovered that young people were far more receptive to the gifts of the Spirit when someone went to a microphone and shared a word without becoming overly emotional or interrupting the flow of the service. He also noticed that people who came to a microphone tended to be more specific and "on message" and delivered in everyday language rather than in old King James English. These simple guidelines opened the door to many more people participating in the gifts of the Spirit.[5]

Another church was led to use microphones for the vocal gifts for a very different reason. This church distributed recordings of their services to shut-ins and to those who were unable to attend a particular service. After listening to the recordings, people would often complain that they couldn't hear what was being said when the vocal gifts were in operation. When they began to use microphones for the vocal gifts, those receiving the recordings could hear what was being said.[6]

We have also been in churches where someone has received a word from the Lord during the week for the church, have written it down, and shared it with the church after having it approved by the pastor or designated leaders.

Over the years we have seen a word of prophecy ministered in each of these ways in churches. In some churches it's been in the traditional way of someone spontaneously sharing the word at an appropriate time in the service. In other churches people have come to a microphone and shared the word the Lord had given them. In some churches a person has written down the word the Lord had given them, given it to the pastor, and the pastor has shared it with the church. Also, in some churches people have verbally shared with the pastor the word the Lord had given them and the pastor has shared it with the church. Whatever the church policy is, flow with it. The important thing is that the word from the Lord gets shared with the church. The means is not as important as the message.

An example of a personal word of prophecy today would be someone saying they have, or feel they may have, "a word from the Lord" for someone. Again, remember a "word from the Lord" is not meant to be directive but rather to confirm what the Lord has already been saying to the individual.

HOW TO BE USED IN THE GIFT OF PROPHECY

Being used in the gift of prophecy starts by being open to being used. If God desires to use you, you will sense it and you will sense God giving you some words. You generally will not get all the words, but only a few words or phrases.

At that point, use what Evangelist Ken Krivohlavek called "the ten-second test." Just hold steady for ten seconds. If the words or phrases are still there, and the time in the service is appropriate, speak them out.

As we mentioned previously, you will get a few words or phrases. As you speak them out, God will give you more words and phrases until the message is complete. Also, as we previously mentioned, in cases where the church policy is to first clear the message with a pastor or church leader, then the whole message may be given.

Also, remember that the word of prophecy in a church setting, and even in a private setting, is to be given at an appropriate time. In a church setting, the appropriate time is not during the middle of a sermon or during someone's solo. An appropriate time is during a pause in the worship time, during a transition time in the service, etc.

A word of prophecy does not need to be given at the very moment someone senses God desiring to use them. If it's God, it will still be there at the appropriate time. Some have mistakenly spoken out at inappropriate times and felt they had to give it right then. No. In order for the gifts to operate decently and in order, not causing confusion, Paul wrote to the Corinthians in 1 Corinthians 14,

"But everything should be done in a fitting and orderly way." (1 Corinthians 14:40, NIV)

"Many assume that those who exercise an utterance gift (a word of prophecy or message in tongues) cannot control themselves and are forced to speak."[7] This is not true. Paul said,

"The spirits of the prophets are subject to the control of the prophets. For God is not a God of disorder but of peace." (1 Corinthians 14:32-33, NIV)

"The idea that people who give an utterance of the Spirit (a word of prophecy or a message in tongues) always speak spontaneously or must blurt it out when they feel the impulse is not biblical."[8] Wait for an appropriate time in the service.

If you have a "prophetic word" for someone, in the same way, wait for the appropriate time and place to share it with them. It may be right at the moment you receive it or it may be later and should be in a normal, conversational way.

For example, if you are in a grocery store and God spoke to you about someone you saw in one of the aisles, how would you use that gift? Hopefully you wouldn't close your eyes, shake, lift your voice, and start to say, "Thus saith the Lord…" That would totally freak people out. Rather, you might approach that person in a humble tone and introduce yourself. Then explain what happened to you as you walked down the aisle. Explain how you believe the Holy Spirit prompted you to say something. Present your message in a sensitive way, aware of your surroundings, and in touch with the person's reactions and response.

REVIEW AND DISCUSSION QUESTIONS

1. Describe what the gift of prophecy is.

2. Describe what the gift of prophecy is not.

3. What is the purpose of the gift of prophecy?

4. How is a message of prophecy received and given?

5. When should a message of prophecy be given?

Chapter Eleven

MESSAGE IN TONGUES

"To another different kinds of tongues."
(1 Corinthians 12:10, NIV)

WHAT IS THE GIFT OF A MESSAGE IN TONGUES?

A message in tongues is a message from God in a language the speaker of the message does not know.

When one speaks in tongues, they speak words that do not originate in the human mind; they come from one's spirit through the Holy Spirit. The Holy Spirit gives the language while the human speaker submits his or her vocal cords for articulation.[1]

An illustration of the words not originating in the human mind would be the experience a woman shared upon receiving the baptism in the Holy Spirit with the initial physical evidence of speaking in tongues. "Analytical by nature, she was extremely curious about what was involved in speaking in tongues. Her first awareness was that the 'unknown words and phrases' did not originate in her mind but from 'somewhere' in her inner being. The unction to speak flowed upward to her vocal cords, not downward from her mind. To push the analysis still further, she picked up a magazine and began to read even as she continued speaking in tongues. Her mind operated on one level; her inner spirit on another."[2]

While this illustration deals with a person speaking in tongues in their personal prayer time, the principle is the same when someone gives a public message in tongues. The message does not originate with the speaker and in the human mind, but is a message from God through a human vessel in a language the speaker does not know.

In 1 Corinthians 14, Paul tells us three things a message in tongues does.

First, a message in tongues edifies the giver of the message in tongues.

"He who speaks in a tongue edifies himself."
(1 Corinthians 14:4, NIV)

Second, a message in tongues edifies the church when the message is interpreted.

"He who prophesies is greater than one who speaks in tongues, unless he interprets, so that the church may be edified." (1 Corinthians 14:5, NIV)

Third, a message in tongues is a sign to the unbeliever.

"Tongues, then, are a sign, not for believers but for unbelievers." (1 Corinthians 14:22, NIV)

WHAT THE GIFT OF A MESSAGE
IN TONGUES IS NOT

A message in tongues is not someone knowing another language. It also is not someone speaking in their prayer language. It can be the same language, but the difference is a Spirit-filled believer can speak in their prayer language whenever they choose, but a message in tongues can only be given when the Holy Spirit desires to use someone in this gift.

It is in this area that people get confused and misinterpret and misapply Scripture. They mistakenly interpret what happened in Acts 2 as being the same as what Paul is writing about in 1 Corinthians 12 and 14. They are not the same thing.

In 1 Corinthians 12:30, Paul writes,

"Do all possess gifts of healing? Do all speak with tongues? Do all interpret?" (1 Corinthians 12:30, ESV)

In 1 Corinthians 12:30, Paul is dealing with congregational tongues, giving a public message in tongues, not with the initial physical evidence of the baptism in the Holy Spirit.[3]

In Acts 2, when people were baptized in the Holy Spirit, they began speaking in other tongues. This was the initial physical evidence that they had received the baptism in the Holy Spirit. This was their own, personal "prayer language" and they could speak in this language whenever they desired now that they were baptized in the Holy Spirit.

This is not what Paul is describing in 1 Corinthians 12 and 14. Here Paul is describing the gift of giving a message in tongues. A message in tongues cannot be done whenever a person desires. A message in tongues can only be given when the Holy Spirit prompts someone to be used in this gift and is to be given at an appropriate time and place.

In fact, not everyone will be used to give a message in tongues. This is what Paul is saying when writing to the Corinthians in 1 Corinthians 12 regarding the gifts of the Holy Spirit,

"Do all speak in tongues?" (1 Corinthians 12:30, NIV)

This was asked in the context of Paul telling the Corinthians, God uses different people in different gifts. Not everyone will be used to give a public message in tongues. However, everyone who is baptized in the Holy Spirit will speak in tongues personally (I explain this in detail in my book on the baptism in the Holy Spirit, *More Power*).

BIBLE EXAMPLES OF THE GIFT OF A MESSAGE IN TONGUES

The clearest references of messages in tongues in the Bible are found in 1 Corinthians chapters 12 and 14. Here Paul is instructing the church in Corinth about what this gift is and how it is to properly function in the church.

No where does Paul say this gift is not to function in the church or to cease functioning in the church. If this gift was not to function in the church, why did Paul take the time to teach the proper use of the gift of tongues in the church?[4] Some erroneously interpret 1 Corinthians 13:8 to mean that this gift is not for today.

In 1 Corinthians 13:8 Paul writes,

"Tongues, they will cease." (1 Corinthians 13:8, NKJV)

Paul also, however, goes on to tell us when this gift will cease a couple of verses later.

"But when that which is perfect has come, then that which is in part will be done away." (1 Corinthians 13:10, NKJV)

The context of this portion of Scripture and what Paul is saying is that now we know in part and we prophesy in part, but when that which is perfect, meaning Jesus, has returned for us, there will be no need for messages in tongues or the other gifts of the Holy Spirit. He will be right there with us! We will be able to communicate with Him face-to-face!

Until Jesus returns for us, we need the gifts of the Holy Spirit; including messages in tongues. Paul writes,

"Do not forbid speaking in tongues." (1 Corinthians 14:39, NIV)

EXAMPLES TODAY OF THE GIFT OF A MESSAGE IN TONGUES

Proper examples today of a message in tongues would be when in a service someone speaks out in an unknown language at an appropriate time.

I will never forget the first time I heard a message in tongues. After having been brought up in a liturgical church and later in an evangelical church, our family then began to visit the nearest Assemblies of God church. I remember a Sunday, it was one of our first visits, when there was pause in the service, and suddenly a lady seated right behind us began to give a message in tongues. I obviously didn't understand what she was saying and wondered what was going on and what was going to happen next. After she stopped, a few moments later someone on the other side of the sanctuary began to speak in English, giving the interpretation, which I could understand. This was my introduction to this gift of the Holy Spirit.

HOW TO BE USED TO GIVE
A MESSAGE IN TONGUES

Being used to give a message in tongues starts by being open to being used. If you sense the Holy Spirit nudging you to be used in this gift, then use the "ten-second test" we mentioned in the previous chapter. Wait ten seconds. If the nudging is still there and it's an appropriate time in the service, speak it out. If the time is not right, wait for an appropriate time and then speak it out.

REVIEW AND DISCUSSION QUESTIONS

1. Describe what the gift of a message in tongues is.

2. Describe what the gift of a message in tongues is not.

3. What are the differences between the gift of giving a message in tongues and the personal evidence of the baptism in the Holy Spirit speaking in tongues?

4. What does a message in tongues do?

5. What are the steps to being used to give a message in tongues?

Chapter Twelve

INTERPRETATION OF TONGUES

∂և∅

"To another the interpretation of tongues."
(1 Corinthians 12:10, NKJV)

WHAT IS THE GIFT OF INTERPRETATION
OF TONGUES?

The gift of interpretation of tongues is an interpretation of the message in tongues that has just been given into the language of those gathered. Notice the wording. It's an interpretation, not a translation. It is not a word-for-word translation, but an interpretation.

This explains why sometimes the interpretation and the message in tongues are not the same length. Sometimes the message in tongues may be longer than the interpretation or vice versa. It's not a word-for-word translation, but rather an interpretation.

An illustration of this difference in length between a message and its interpretation would be when Daniel interpreted God's handwriting on the wall to Belshazzar. Daniel used three sentences to interpret the meaning of the four words God wrote on the wall.

> *"Then from His presence the hand was sent, and this writing was inscribed. And this is the writing that was inscribed: Mene, Mene, Tekel, and Parsin. This is the interpretation of the matter: Mene, God has numbered the days of your kingdom and brought it to an end; Tekel, you have been weighed in the balances and found wanting; Peres, your kingdom is divided and given to the Medes and Persians."*
> (Daniel 5:24-28, ESV)

WHAT THE GIFT OF INTERPRETATION OF TONGUES IS NOT

The gift of the interpretation of tongues is not guessing what the message was. Neither is this gift knowing another language. It also is not planning out ahead of time with the one who gave the message in tongues. It's God giving an individual an interpretation of the message in tongues in a language those gathered understand but where the individual does not know the language the message in tongues was given in.

BIBLE EXAMPLES OF THE GIFT OF INTERPRETAION OF TONGUES

In 1 Corinthians 14 we find references to the operation of the gift of the interpretation of tongues and its importance. Without this gift, a message in tongues will not benefit or edify the church. No one will understand what was said through the message in tongues.

"He who prophesies is greater than one who speaks in tongues, unless he interprets, so that the church may be edified." (1 Corinthians 14:5, NIV)

"For this reason anyone who speaks in a tongue (gives a message in tongues) should pray that he may interpret what he says... If you are praising God with your spirit, how can one who finds himself among those who do not understand say 'Amen' to your thanksgiving, since he does not know what you are saying? You may be giving thanks well enough, but the other man is not edified." (1 Corinthians 14:13-17, NIV)

"When you come together, everyone has a hymn, or a word of instruction, a revelation, a tongue or an interpretation. All of these must be done for the strengthening of the church." (1 Corinthians 14:26, NIV)

"If anyone speaks in a tongue, two or at the most three should speak, one at a time, and someone must interpret." (1 Corinthians 14:27, NIV)

These verses all illustrate the operation of the gift of the interpretation of tongues in the Early Church and the importance of this gift.

EXAMPLES OF THE GIFT OF INTERPRETATION OF TONGUES TODAY

The gift of the interpretation of tongues is still needed and can be a great blessing and benefit to the church today.

Earlier, in chapter 7, I told the beginning of our story of going to our first pastorate. After candidating that Easter

Sunday we returned back to Minneapolis to finish our last month of Bible college. A few days after we returned back to Minneapolis, we were notified by the church we had been selected to be their new pastor. We were so excited. We already had a pastorate and had not even finished Bible college yet. The plan was that we would finish our studies at Bible college and then we would move to our new pastorate.

When we excitedly told people where we had been elected as the new pastor, however, the response often was not favorable. People questioned our sanity and wondered if we knew what we were doing.

After hearing people questioning our soon going to our first pastorate, I was beginning to wonder, *What have we done? What have we gotten ourselves into? What's going to happen to us?*

I still vividly remember a Sunday morning at the church we regularly attended while going to Bible college. During the worship time these questions were rolling over in my mind. Just as I was asking these questions in my mind, there was a pause in the worship service. Someone gave a message in tongues, which of course I didn't understand. Then a few moments later there was an interpretation of the message in tongues. The interpretation was, "Preach the Word, believe the promises, and I will fill your house." Just as I had been asking the questions in my mind, there was the message in tongues and the interpretation of the message in tongues. It was as if God was answering my questions!

That bolstered my faith and was an instrument in the gift of faith God gave us as we went to our first pastorate.

And guess what? God did exactly what He said He would do. Later in the book I'll tell you what God did and how He did it.

We need the voice gifts of the Holy Spirit! A message in tongues in a service does no good, however, unless it's interpreted. No one will understand it unless it's interpreted.

HOW TO BE USED IN THE GIFT OF INTERPRETATION OF TONGUES

When a message in tongues has been given, be open to being used. If you sense God perhaps wanting to use you, you will sense God giving you a few words. You generally will not get all the words at this point, only a few.

Then use the "ten-second test." Wait ten seconds to see if the prompting and words are still there. If they are, then begin to speak them. As you speak the words, more words will be given to you until the interpretation is complete.

If it's a large church and the policy is to go to a designated person, then first share with them the gist of the interpretation, and if approved, then go to a microphone and give the interpretation. Follow the protocol of your church's leadership.

OTHER BIBLE GUIDELINES REGARDING THE VOICE GIFTS

In 1 Corinthians 14:27-33, Paul describes some additional information and guidelines regarding the voice gifts of the Holy Spirit.

1. **In a service there are to be at most three messages in tongues and only one at a time.**

   "If anyone speaks in a tongue, two or at the most three should speak, one at a time." (1 Corinthians 14:27, NIV)

   Some have interpreted it to mean two or three at a time, meaning two or three in one part of the service and then perhaps two or three later in the service.

   Another interpretation I have heard is that any over three are a continuation of the previous one.

   Personally, I take it to mean what it says, two or three at the most and one at a time. In reality, however, the issue today in most cases is not going over three but rather to have even one.

2. **Someone must interpret.**

   "And someone must interpret." (1 Corinthians 14:27, NIV)

   If there is a message in tongues given, there needs to be an interpretation given so the message can be understood.

   I remember a service in our first pastorate where there was a message in tongues. The church had many new believers and the gifts of the Holy Spirit were new to them. Previously when someone had given a message in tongues, the only two people they had ever heard give an interpretation of a message in tongues were Beth and another lady in the church. As I recall, that morning one of them was ministering in the nursery and the other one in the children's church. Later I heard one of the new believers say they were getting ready to go get either Beth or the other lady to come in and give the interpretation. Before they had a chance, however, God used someone else to give the interpretation.

It was a learning experience for the church. They knew the message needed to be interpreted but hadn't realized yet that God can use people in a gift they have never been used in before.

3. **If there is no one to interpret, the speaker should keep quiet.**

   "If there is no interpreter, the speaker should keep quiet in the church and speak to himself and God." (1 Corinthians 14:28, NIV)

   Each public message in tongues in a service needs to be interpreted.

   The one who gives the message in tongues should pray that they will be given the interpretation.

   "Anyone who speaks in a tongue should pray that he may interpret what he says." (1 Corinthians 14:13, NIV)

   If there is no one to interpret or the one giving the message in tongues is not willing to give the interpretation, they should keep quiet. Each public message in tongues needs to be interpreted.

4. **At most there should be three prophecies.**

   "Two or three prophets should speak, and the others should weigh carefully what is said." (1 Corinthians 14:29, NIV)

Some have interpreted this to mean only two or three different individuals should give words of prophecy in any given service, but the number of prophecies can be more than three.

Others have interpreted this to mean that any prophecies over three are just a continuation of the previous one.

I prefer to just take it at face value to mean two or three prophecies in any given service unless it is obvious that those over three are just finishing or a continuation of the third one.

Today the issue in most churches, however, is not an issue of going over three prophecies in a service, but to have even one.

5. **If someone is giving a prophecy and someone else starts — the first one should stop.**

   "Two or three prophets should speak... And if a revelation comes to someone who is sitting down, the first speaker should stop. For you can all prophesy in turn so that everyone may be instructed and encouraged." (1 Corinthians 14:29-31, NIV)

6. **The spirits of the prophets are subject to the prophets.**

   "The spirits of the prophets are subject to the control of the prophets." (1 Corinthians 14:32, NIV)

A person being used in a gift of the Holy Spirit is not out of control. They can stop if necessary as referred to in the previous point. Also, as mentioned previously, a person can wait for an appropriate time to share their gift.

7. **Everything is to be done in an orderly way.**

"For God is not a God of disorder but of peace." (1 Corinthians 14:33, NIV)

"But everything should be done in a fitting and orderly way." (1 Corinthians 14:40, NIV)

Paul never tells the Corinthians, or us today, to stop the gifts but rather to manifest the gifts in an orderly way.

PRACTICAL GUIDELINES FOR LEADERS REGARDING THE VOICE GIFTS

1. **What to say after a manifestation of the voice gifts.**

After a voice gift has been manifested in a service or Bible study, the one in leadership should take the opportunity to make it a teaching moment. For the benefit of visitors who may be present or for those unfamiliar with the gifts of the Holy Spirit, briefly explain what has just happened.

An example of what could be said is:

"What has just happened is what the Bible refers to as a message in tongues and an interpretation of the message in tongues (or prophecy if it was the gift of prophecy). These gifts are described in the Bible in 1 Corinthians chapters 12 and 14. Through these gifts we have been encouraged to...."[1]

Then give the essence of what the message was and encourage and give opportunity to respond to the message. Don't ignore the manifestation of the gift and rush on to the next part of the service. Use the manifestation of the voice gift as a teaching and ministry opportunity.

2. **What could be said when an interpretation did not follow a message in tongues.**

"What we have just heard was a vocal gift of tongues described in 1 Corinthians 12 and 14. We know from Scripture that a public message in tongues without an interpretation is not the proper function of that gift. That does not always mean that the message in tongues was not from the Lord. It may mean that the person who was to give the interpretation did not obey. Or, it could mean that the speaker was offering praise to God and was not to be interpreted and was not for the whole congregation. Let's remember that just because the gifts may be used imperfectly sometimes, it does not mean we should not allow their use at all. Let's continue to grow in our understanding of how to be used of God in the ministry of the gifts. In spite of our frailties and mistakes, God will be faithful to continue to speak to us."[2]

If you ignore what happened, people will leave the service or Bible study confused and with questions.

3. **What could be said in public correction.**

Many things are not serious enough to be corrected publicly and can be and should be corrected privately. Some of the reasons public correction might be needed are: contradiction of the doctrines, principles, and facts of Scripture; misrepresentation of the character of God; presenting an unbalanced truth; or when private correction has failed. Also, public correction does not always have to follow immediately after the vocal gift has been given. An interval in the service can help the leader formulate a response.

Sometimes, however, the leader should not wait. Such as when what is being said or the spirit in which it is being said is so bad it must be stopped. Or perhaps the timing of the vocal gift interrupts the flow of the service.[3]

When public correction is needed, an example of what could be said would be:

"We are a Pentecostal church, and we appreciate the gifts of the Spirit and encourage their use. But all supernatural vocal gifts are to be judged by the Word. And one thing that was said about God does not match what the Scripture says about Him. (Point out the error, and contrast it with Scripture.) We are always in good order to stick to what the Scripture says."[4]

As we mentioned earlier, if you ignore what happened, people will leave the service or Bible study confused and with questions.

REVIEW AND DISCUSSION QUESTIONS

1. Describe what the gift of interpretation of tongues is.

2. Describe what the gift of interpretation of tongues is not.

3. Describe how to be used to give an interpretation of a message in tongues.

4. Explain why many times the length of the message in tongues and the interpretation of the message in tongues are not the same.

5. Explain what "the spirits of the prophets are subject to the control of the prophets" means.

Chapter Thirteen

GENERAL KEYS – GUIDELINES AND CONCLUSION

⸛⸕

GENERAL KEYS AND GUIDELINES

1. **Be baptized in the Holy Spirit**. The baptism in the Holy Spirit makes all the gifts available to the believer and greatly increases the likelihood of being used in the gifts. If you have not been baptized in the Holy Spirit or want to know more, I recommend getting my book, *More Power*, from Amazon in either the paperback or Kindle version. If you have been seeking the baptism in the Holy Spirit but have not yet received, keep seeking. He will baptize you in the Holy Spirit! The baptism in the Holy Spirit is not necessary for salvation but it is necessary to reach one's full potential. Without the baptism in the Holy Spirit, we will not be all we can be nor will we do all we can do. With the baptism in the Holy Spirit we will be more than we are. This includes being used in the gifts of the Holy Spirit.

2. **Stay filled with the Holy Spirit.** An experience of being baptized in the Holy Spirit years ago that isn't fresh in our life today is a wonderful historical memory but it doesn't help us with everyday living today. We need to stay filled with the Holy Spirit. Take time to pray in the Spirit every day. Praying in the Spirit keeps the experience fresh and keeps us in tune with the Spirit. Also, praying in the Spirit makes us sensitive to the Spirit, enabling us to hear the voice of the Spirit more clearly, which then enables us to be used in the gifts of the Holy Spirit.

3. **Desire and pray to be used.** Make yourself available by desiring and praying to be used in the gifts of the Holy Spirit.

4. **Be open and alert to being used.** We often miss God wanting to use us as just a passing thought. We need to be sensitive and alert to the promptings of the Holy Spirit. A key to being used in the gifts of the Holy Spirit is to be open and alert.

5. **Don't be afraid of making mistakes.** In an article Warren Bullock wrote he said, "Following the voice of the Spirit is a skill that is honed through both prayer and error. Prayer increases one's sensitivities to the Spirit, and error helps you know when you missed His direction. You learn and grow from both. Someone said, 'We will never be used if we're not willing to fail.' "[1] It's been said, "I'd rather be a wet water walker than a dry boat sitter," referring to Peter walking on the water in Matthew 14. Being used in the gifts of the Holy Spirit is in many ways like walking on water.

6. **Step out in faith.** Unless we step out in faith, we will miss the opportunity to have been used in a gift of the Holy Spirit. God won't make us be used. We must step out in faith. Peter first desired to walk on the water. We need to desire to be used. Then Peter had to have an invitation from Jesus. We need to have a prompting of the Holy Spirit that He desires to use us. Then Peter had to step out of the boat in order to walk on the water. If he didn't step out in faith, he never would have walked on the water. If we don't step out in faith, we will miss the opportunity to be used in the gift of the Holy Spirit God desires to use us in.

7. **Be submissive to the leadership of the church.** Whatever way the church leadership desires to function in the gifts of the Holy Spirit, be submissive. The gifts of the Holy Spirit were not to be a point and source of confusion or division. If you have questions or concerns, talk to the leaders in a Christ-like way. If they don't believe the gifts are for today or are not open to the gifts, then prayerfully consider leaving and finding a church that is. "Any church that discourages or prohibits the expression of spiritual gifts, that church is giving up a powerful spiritual advantage."[2]

8. **Be open to constructive correction.** We need to be open to constructive correction. Being used in the gifts of the Holy Spirit is a learning process and sometimes we may need constructive correction. Be open to it. I recall an incident in our second pastorate when a lady and her husband began attending our church. She already was a believer and Spirit-filled when they came. She began to be used in the voice gifts in the services. Many were "right on" but some were not. They were

not serious enough to have to correct publicly, so I contacted her privately to endeavor to lovingly correct her. Her response basically was, "I'll do what I believe the Spirit wants me to." I said to her, "We have had this discussion in private to correct this, but if this continues, the next correction will be public." She left the church and we never saw her again. A few weeks later a neighboring pastor called me and sarcastically said, "Thanks a lot for sending Sue (name changed) to us." I told him I didn't send her and then told him what had happened. He said she was now doing the same thing at his church. She was an example of someone not being open to constructive correction. "The acid test of spirituality is whether or not a person can receive correction."[3] Anyone who has been erroneous on a continual basis should be asked to submit their message before giving it to a more mature and proven person or church leadership, who have been accurate in being used in this gift. Those who refuse to submit to their insight should be prohibited from speaking because their "prophetic" words could be detrimental to the church.[4]

9. **Let God use you in a small-group setting to start.** For many people it's easier to do something in a small-group setting rather than a large group. This can apply to being used in the gifts of the Holy Spirit also. It may be easier for some to step out in faith in a small group when first starting to be used in the gifts.

CONCLUSION

The story is told about Yogi Berra, the famous Hall of Fame catcher for the New York Yankees, and Hank Aaron, the famous Hall of Fame player for the Atlanta Braves. The Yankees and Braves were playing against each other and Hank Aaron came up to bat. Yogi Berra was in his usual position as catcher. One of the tasks of the catcher, in addition to catching the pitches, is to try to distract the batter by saying things to the batter, being they are positioned right behind the batter. As Berra is chattering away at Aaron, trying to distract him, he says, "Hey Aaron, you can't read the writing, your bat is upside down" (with a wooden bat you are always supposed to hold it facing the writing on the bat; if you don't, the bat may break when you hit the ball). Aaron refused to get distracted. The pitcher threw the next pitch and Aaron hit the ball over the fence for a home run. After Aaron had run around the bases and crossed home plate, as he was walking back to the dugout, he turned toward Berra and said, "Hey Berra, I didn't come here to read." Hank Aaron knew what he was there for.

We need to know what we are here for. We are here to live for Christ and serve God; and He has made available to us everything we need, which includes His power tools, the gifts of the Holy Spirit.

In Scripture we are encouraged to:

- know about the gifts
- desire the gifts
- be used in the gifts

The world is hungry for the supernatural. They look everywhere for the supernatural. They go to psychics, fortunetellers, horoscopes, witchcraft, etc. — all in the search for the supernatural.

The church has been given supernatural tools: the gifts of the Holy Spirit. These gifts worked in the Early Church, even in a non-Judeo-Christian culture, and they are still available and work today. They are God's power tools for life and ministry.

After graduating from Bible college, Beth and I moved to west central Minnesota to begin pastoring our first church. We stepped out on a new adventure, going to what the district superintendent had called "a wonderful opportunity," wondering what we had gotten ourselves into.

As I mentioned in an earlier chapter, just as I had been asking in my mind in a service at the church we were attending while going to Bible college, *What have we done? What's going to happen to us?*; there was a message in tongues and an interpretation of the message in tongues. The message was short and to the point — "Preach the Word, believe the promises, and I will fill your house."

We moved to west central Minnesota and began our ministry, endeavoring the best we could to do what God had said. And for no explainable reason, except God doing what God said He would do, He did exactly what He said He would do. It wasn't us, but it was Him!

After we had been there a while a young family moved into our area and became a part of our church. They were already believers. Their moving into our area was a miracle in itself. They had no relatives in the area. They had no job waiting for them in the area. They had no friends in the area. They had no reason to move there except God was placing them there to be a key to fulfilling what He had said months earlier through the gifts of the Holy Spirit.

The husband, Jim (name changed), needed to find a job. Jobs were not abundant in this small town of 750 people, but he crossed paths with Steve (name changed), owner of a local painting business. He painted houses, barns, etc., and needed someone to help him in the painting business. Steve, in addition to being a painter by profession, was also a rock musician and sang in bars and clubs.

Jim began to work for Steve and would tell Steve about Jesus when he had the opportunity as they worked together. Steve wasn't very interested. In fact, he had a name for all the people of our church. He would refer to them as "Juoni's Moonies" (my last name and a cult called the Moonies). Steve didn't seem very interested, but Jim would share the message of Jesus whenever he could. He was not pushy but shared as he had the opportunity. Weeks went by, perhaps even months, but Steve didn't seem really interested.

After a period of time had passed, one Sunday morning as I looked out at the congregation as the service began, there was Steve sitting out in the audience. He sat throughout the worship time, the message, and the altar time, and he left. We didn't see him for weeks, but Jim continued to work for Steve and to tell him about Jesus and answer his questions.

Several weeks later, on a Sunday morning as the service began, I looked out and there was Steve again. Sitting in the same area, he sat through the worship time, the message, and the altar time, and he left. We again didn't see him for weeks, but Jim continued to work for Steve and tell him about Jesus and answer his questions.

Weeks later, as the Sunday morning service was beginning, I looked out and there was Steve again, sitting in the same area. On this particular Sunday morning we were having communion in the service. As we prepared to serve communion, I always reminded the people that communion is a service where followers of Jesus remind themselves of what Jesus has done for them. We also always said, "If you are here today and have not given your life to Christ, you can do it this morning right where you are at. You can ask Jesus to forgive you of your sins and make a commitment to follow Him."

That Sunday morning Steve asked Jesus to come into his life, to forgive him of his sins, and he committed his life to follow Jesus. After that he got baptized in water and baptized in the Holy Spirit. In the following days he also brought his wife and two teenage daughters to church and each of them gave their lives to Christ. They all were musical, so we instantly had a worship team! We just had to redirect their music.

I will never forget the day Steve came to me and asked, "Pastor, can I bring my 'outlaw friends' to church?" I said, "Sure." He said, "What if the church people won't accept them?" I said, "You just bring the outlaws, I'll deal with the church people."

He started to bring his friends and they started to give their lives to Christ. They also had friends; they brought them, and they started to give their lives to Christ. Soon the people who were already part of the church caught on and realized, *We can do this too; we've got friends.* They started to bring their friends and they were coming to Christ and becoming a part of the church.

Soon the existing building was becoming too small to accommodate everyone. We had to expand the building to basically triple the seating capacity. In addition to expanding the sanctuary, however, we also needed more space for Sunday school classes and other ministries to accommodate the growing numbers. The best way we could solve the problem was for us to move out of the three-bedroom apartment we were living in (that was attached to the church) and buy a house in town. So we moved out of the apartment and bought a house.

Do you see what happened? God had said, through the gifts of the Holy Spirit, "Preach the Word, believe the promises, and I will fill your house." He literally did exactly what He said He would do! In fact, I thought He meant He would fill the sanctuary, which He did. But He was much more literal. God literally filled our house, our apartment. He did exactly what He said He would do!

The gifts of the Holy Spirit are wonderful tools for life and ministry. I recall reading an article by a veteran missionary who said ten months after he first went to India he became very discouraged and was ready to come home. He couldn't convince the Hindus and Muslims about Jesus. They were very kind and loved to talk about religion, but they were not interested in his message about Jesus. In fact, the Hindus and Muslims tried to convert him and his wife to their religions. It was then he realized that without the supernatural he couldn't prove what he believed.

The gifts of the Holy Spirit give us the supernatural. They are God's power tools for life and ministry. Our part is, we have to step out in faith as the Holy Spirit prompts us and desires to use us. Let's allow the Holy Spirit to work through us, confirming our message about Jesus.

"We have been saved and filled with the Holy Spirit for a purpose beyond self-gratification."[5] Self-gratification is a dead end. Through the Holy Spirit, the Pentecostal church has received supernatural gifts and resources to perfect the church for ministry and empower it to impact the world for Christ.

Let's not be content to live without the supernatural. John Wesley said,

> "My fear is not that our great movement…will eventually cease to exist or one day die from the earth. My fear is that our people will become content to live without the fire, the power, the excitement, the supernatural element that makes us great."[6]

While John Wesley was speaking of his denomination, we can apply it to us today. Let's not be content to live without the supernatural element of the gifts of the Holy Spirit. Let's desire spiritual gifts, the "power tools" that God has made available for life and ministry.

The Bible says,

> *"Then the disciples went out and preached everywhere, and the Lord worked with them and confirmed his word by the signs that accompanied it."* (Mark 16:20, NIV)

REVIEW AND DISCUSSION QUESTIONS

1. Why is staying filled with the Holy Spirit important?

2. How does a person stayed filled with the Holy Spirit?

3. What is the proper way to handle disagreements with church leadership?

4. What is the proper way to handle constructive correction?

5. Why is the supernatural important?

ENDNOTES

CHAPTER ONE

1. Randy Hurst, *Divine Order* (Springfield, MO: Access Group, 2009), from "Forward" by George O. Wood, page 11.
2. Charles Crabtree, *The Pentecostal Priority* (Springfield, MO: National Decade of Harvest, 1993), page 16.
3. Ed Stetzer, complete article "Why are Pentecostals Growing in Number?" found at churchleaders.com.
4. Don Cox, *The Other 8 Gifts* (Waterloo, IA: Don Cox, 1975), page 66.
5. Ibid.

CHAPTER TWO

1. Donald Stamps, *Fire Bible: English Standard Version* (Peabody, MA: Hendrickson Publishers Marketing, 2011), page 2048.
2. Ibid., page 1517.
3. Ken Krivohlavek, *Desire Spiritual Gifts* (Springfield, MO: Ken Krivohlavek, 1976), page 2.
4. Verna M. Linzey, *The Gifts of the Spirit* (Lake Mary, FL: Charisma House, 2014), page 8.
5. Ibid., page 5.
6. Ibid., pages 5-7.

7. Randy Hurst, *Divine Order* (Springfield, MO: Access Group, 2009), from "Power and Propriety" by Randy Hurst, page 17.

8. Warren D. Bullock, *When the Spirit Speaks* (Springfield, MO: Gospel Publishing House, 2009), page 44.

9. Verna M. Linzey, *The Gifts of the Spirit* (Lake Mary, FL: Charisma House, 2014), page xxi.

10. Stamps, *Fire Bible: English Standard Version*, page 427.

11. Ibid., page 1958.

12. Thomas Trask and David Womack, *Back to the Altar* (Springfield, MO: Gospel Publishing House, 1994), pages 75-76.

13. Ibid., pages 74-75.

14. Don Cox, *The Other 8 Gifts* (Waterloo, IA: Don Cox, 1975), page 5.

15. Stamps, *Fire Bible: English Standard Version*, page 1930.

CHAPTER THREE

1. Jeff Leake, *Power for Life* (Springfield, MO: Gospel Publishing House, 2017), pages 83-86.

2. George O. Wood, "A Waterline of Another Kind – Six Marks of a Pentecostal Church," *Enrichment Journal* (Springfield, MO: Gospel Publishing House, 5/6/2011).

3. Jeff Leake, *Power for Life* (Springfield, MO: Gospel Publishing House, 2017), page 116.

CHAPTER FOUR

1. Verna M. Linzey, *The Gifts of the Spirit* (Lake Mary, FL: Charisma House, 2014), page 53.

2. Ibid., page 54.

CHAPTER FIVE

1. Ron Auch Sr., from message preached, pastor of Prayer House Assembly of God in Kenosha, WI.

2. Ron Auch Sr., "Acts of the Holy Spirit" message, pastor of Prayer House Assembly of God in Kenosha, WI.

3. Verna M. Linzey, *The Gifts of the Spirit* (Lake Mary, FL: Charisma House, 2014), page 56.

4. Larry Sparks and Troy Anderson, "The Healing Miracles Preacher," *Charisma* (Lake Mary, FL: Charisma Media, March 2015), page 21.

5. Joni Jones, "Holy Spirit Encounters," *Ministry Today* (Lake Mary, FL: Charisma Media, June 2018), page 61.

CHAPTER SIX

1. Verna M. Linzey, *The Gifts of the Spirit* (Lake Mary, FL: Charisma House, 2014), page 86.

2. Ibid., page 88.

3. Ibid., page 82.

4. Ibid., page 85

5. Donald Stamps, *Fire Bible: English Standard Version* (Peabody, MA: Hendrickson Publishers Marketing, 2011), page 1686.

6. Rodney M. Howard-Browne, *Flowing in the Holy Spirit* (Shippensburg, PA: Destiny Image, 2000), pages 115-116.

CHAPTER SEVEN

1. Verna M. Linzey, *The Gifts of the Spirit* (Lake Mary, FL: Charisma House, 2014), pages 61-62.

2. Ibid., page 62.

3. Smith Wigglesworth, *Ever Increasing Faith* (Springfield, MO: Gospel Publishing House, 1924), pages 138-139.

4. Rodney M. Howard-Browne, *Flowing in the Holy Spirit* (Shippensburg, PA: Destiny Image, 2000), pages 14-15.

CHAPTER EIGHT

1. *The Gifts & Fruit of the Holy Spirit* (Springfield, MO: Gospel Publishing House, 2010), page 6.

2. Ibid.

3. Verna M. Linzey, *The Gifts of the Spirit* (Lake Mary, FL: Charisma House, 2014), page 68.

CHAPTER NINE

1. Verna M. Linzey, *The Gifts of the Spirit* (Lake Mary, FL: Charisma House, 2014), page 71.

2. Ibid., page 72.

3. Cathy Ketcher, *Marvels and Miracles* (Springfield, MO: Gospel Publishing House, 2014), page 48.

4. Ibid., page 57.

CHAPTER TEN

1. Charles Crabtree, *The Pentecostal Priority* (Springfield, MO: National Decade of Harvest, 1993), page 24.

2. Rodney M. Howard-Browne, *Flowing in the Holy Spirit* (Shippensburg, PA: Destiny Image, 2000), pages 31.

3. Jack Hayford, *New Spirit Filled Life Bible,* (Nashville, TN: Thomas Nelson Publishers, 2002), page 1531

4. Jeff Leake, *Power for Life* (Springfield, MO: Gospel Publishing House, 2017), pages 105-106.

5. Randy Hurst, *Divine Order* (Springfield, MO: Access Group, 2009), from "God Can Speak Through Microphones" by James T. Bradford, pages 37- 39.

6. Ibid., from "Climate of Order," by Tim Enloe, page 53.

7. Ibid., from "Power and Propriety," by Randy Hurst, page 22.

8. Ibid., page 20.

CHAPTER ELEVEN

1. Verna M. Linzey, *The Gifts of the Spirit* (Lake Mary, FL: Charisma House, 2014), page 92.

2. Ibid.

3. Charles Crabtree, *The Pentecostal Priority* (Springfield, MO: National Decade of Harvest, 1993), page 76.
4. Ibid., page 77.

CHAPTER TWELVE

1. Warren D. Bullock, *When the Spirit Speaks* (Springfield, MO: Gospel Publishing House, 2009), page 83.
2. Ibid., page 85.
3. Ibid., pages 76-78.
4. Ibid., page 86.

CHAPTER THIRTEEN

1. Warren D. Bullock, *Live* (Springfield, MO: Gospel Publishing House, 2009), page 7.
2. Randy Hurst, *Divine Order* (Springfield, MO: Access Group, 2009), from "Orderly Ministry Blesses the Church," by Thomas E. Trask, page 32.
3. Ibid., from "Forward" by George O. Wood, page 13
4. Verna M. Linzey, *The Gifts of the Spirit* (Lake Mary, FL: Charisma House, 2014), page 79.
5. Charles Crabtree, *The Pentecostal Priority* (Springfield, MO: National Decade of Harvest, 1993), page 12.
6. Scott Wilson and John Bates, *Spread the Fire* (Springfield, MO: Gospel Publishing House, 2016), page 169.

ABOUT THE AUTHOR

Bill was born and raised in the Upper Peninsula of Michigan and made a commitment of his life to Christ at the age of ten. He graduated from Northern Michigan University in Marquette, MI, with a bachelor's degree in marketing and worked in retail management for three years. While working in the business world, Bill met Beth. They were married and have served the Lord together ever since.

After three years in retail management, Bill left the business world to fulfill God's call to the ministry by going to North Central University in Minneapolis, MN. Upon graduation with a bachelor's degree in pastoral studies, Bill accepted a pastorate in Minnesota as lead pastor at their first church. During their time there the church grew and entered a building program to triple the size of the sanctuary as people were coming to Christ and being baptized in the Holy Spirit. After eight years as lead pastor, Bill resigned to accept the call to his second pastorate.

The second pastorate was located in Wisconsin and Bill served as lead pastor there for twelve years. During that time they again saw people come to Christ and baptized in the Holy Spirit as the church reached out with multiple outreaches. During that time, Bill and Beth also began to go out ministering on missions trips in America and overseas, bringing church groups with them.

In 1998, God changed the direction of their ministry and called them to travel as evangelists. Since then they have traveled across America and overseas, ministering on the baptism in the Holy Spirit and how to live a Spirit-filled life.

You can find more information about Bill and Beth and their ministry by going to their website at:

billjuonifreshfire.com

ALSO WRITTEN BY BILL JUONI

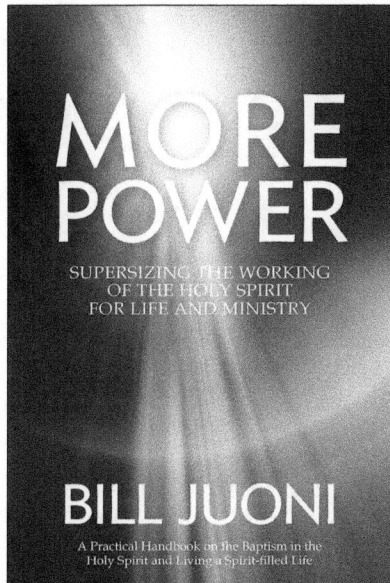

Available from Amazon.com in paperback and Kindle ebook

www.ingramcontent.com/pod-product-compliance
Lightning Source LLC
LaVergne TN
LVHW051414080426
835508LV00022B/3078